The TIME FOR PRAYER Program

זְמַן לִתְפִילָה

BOOK 3: עֲמִידָה

Dina Maiben and Hillary Zana

A.R.E. Publishing, Inc.

Denver, Colorado

Dear Students,

בְּרוּכִים הַבָּאִים!

Welcome to Book 3 of the זְמַן לִתְפִלָה Program. This year you will:

- continue to practice your reading skills
- continue learning how to pray
- discuss some important ideas about God and prayer
- explore some key Hebrew prayer words
- add to your treasury of Hebrew words.

In this book you will study the עֲמִידָה. The Rabbis taught that the עֲמִידָה is so important that this part of the service is like appearing before God's royal court. So polish up your reading skills, roll out the red carpet, and get ready for the עֲמִידָה.

רָצָה	שָׁנָה	מַצָּה	חַלָּה	יָד	אַבָּא	דָּג	שַׁבָּת	**.1**
שִׁשִׁי	תִּיק	אֲגַם	דָּמִי	יָשָׁר	בֹּקֶר	דָּגָן	הַשַׁבָּת	**.2**
צִיצִית	קָטִין	פְּקָה	מִיָּד	דִּינָה	הָאִשָׁה	כֻּתָּה	אִמָּא	**.3**
צָלוּם	יָדַיִם	מַיִם	אֲנִין	אַדִּיר	יַגִּיד	תָּמִיד	אֲנִי	**.4**
חֲנֻכָּה	חָמֵשׁ	חֻפָּה	פָּקִיד	גָּדוֹל	קָדוֹשׁ	שׁוּרָה	שׁוּק	**.5**
בַּחוּרָה	פָּגוּל	נִגּוּן	יַבָּשָׁה	פָּנִים	רַחוּם	טִפָּה	הַגָּדָה	**.6**
שְׁלוּמִים	אֱמִינוּת	קַשָׁרוּת	קָצוּר	אַחֲרִית	פּוּרִים	בַּיִת	יַיִן	**.7**

Hitting the Mark

The beginning of the year is a good time to set some goals, and to reflect on what we did in the previous year. During the High Holy Days, we often think about having "missed the mark" in the past year. Now that you are beginning a new year in Hebrew school, practice "hitting the mark" with your Hebrew reading skills.

Play this game with a friend or in class teams. Taking turns, read any word on the dart board. If you read it correctly, you score the number of points written in that space. Mark off the words as you read them correctly. When all the words have been read, total your scores.

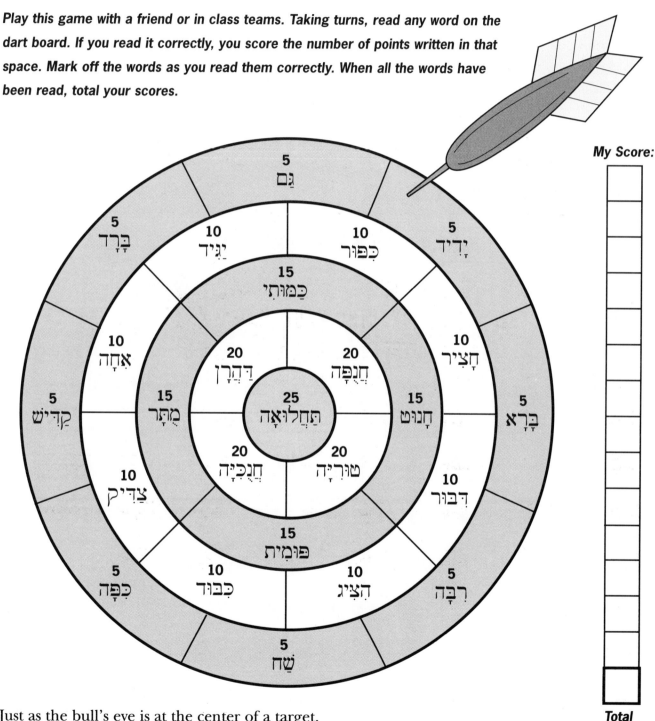

My Score:

Total

Just as the bull's eye is at the center of a target, the עֲמִידָה is central to every Jewish service.

אֲדֹנָי מֶלֶךְ

Imagine living at a time of powerful kings and queens. You have been chosen to present your community's requests before the royal court.

When a person appears before royalty, there are certain formalities that must be followed. First, you enter the royal presence and bow. You introduce yourself to the court. You acknowledge all of the ruler's great deeds and explain how these have benefitted the subjects of the land. Then, humbly, you present your requests. You end your presentation with thanks to the court for having listened to you. Finally, you take your leave from the royal presence.

In the Talmud, Rabbi Chanina says that reciting the עֲמִידָה is like presenting a set of petitions to God's royal court. You begin by entering God's presence. You remind God of who you are and acknowledge all the wonderful things that God does for us. Then you make a series of requests, thank God, and take your leave.

Climb the ladder of the עֲמִידָה.

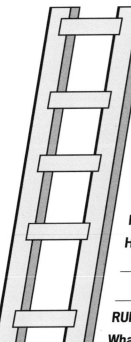

RUNG 5: TAKING YOUR LEAVE
How would you leave God with a favorable impression?

_____

RUNG 4: THANKSGIVING
What did God do that you are thankful for?

_____

RUNG 3: YOUR HUMBLE REQUESTS
What things would you ask God to do?

_____

RUNG 2: PRAISE FOR THE RULER
How would you remind God of who you are? For what things would you praise God?

_____

_____

RUNG 1: ENTERING THE ROYAL PRESENCE — MAKE A GOOD IMPRESSION
What would you do to make this good impression?

_____

With this format in mind, it's time to take the first steps into God's court.

INTRODUCTION

אֲדֹנָי שְׂפָתַי תִּפְתָּח

KEY WORD: שָׂפָה

The עֲמִידָה begins and ends with reminders about the power of language. In its opening line, we ask God to help us use our speech for good, rather than evil purposes.

Many Hebrew words appear in different forms. The word at the end of each line comes from the opening phrase of the עֲמִידָה. Practice reading these prayer words in all their forms.

אֲדֹנָי	אֲדוֹנַי	יְיָ
שְׂפָתַי	שְׂפַת	שָׂפָה
תִּפְתָּח	פָּתַח	פָּתַח
וּפִי	פִּי	פֶּה
תְּהִלָּתֶךָ	תְּהִלַּת	תְּהִלָּה

Now, practice reading the Introduction to the עֲמִידָה.

Adonai open my lips,

and my mouth shall tell Your praise.

אֲדֹנָי שְׂפָתַי תִּפְתָּח,

וּפִי יַגִּיד תְּהִלָּתֶךָ.

Rabbi Yonatan taught: "There are four languages. Roman is the best for battle. Greek is the best for song. Persian is the best for mourning, and Hebrew is the best for prayer."

(Midrash on Psalms, 1:398)

אוֹצַר מִלִּים
A TREASURY OF WORDS

Fill in the missing translation.

Language =		שָׂפָה
_____ =		שָׂפוֹת
The Hebrew Language =		הַשָׂפָה הָעִבְרִית
Holy Language (עִבְרִית) =		לְשׁוֹן הַקֹּדֶשׁ
Evil Speech (Gossip) =		לְשׁוֹן הָרָע

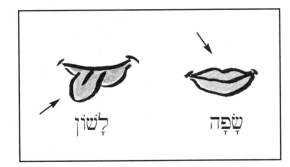

לָשׁוֹן   שָׂפָה

מִיכָאֶל אִיז אַ מֶענטש.
(Michael is a mentsch.)

מַזָל בּוּאֵינוּ!
(Mazal tov!)

שָׁלוֹם!

אִידִישׁ   לַאדִינוֹ   עִבְרִית   סַבְתָּא   סַבָּא

הַשָׂפוֹת שֶׁל הָעוֹלָם

Match each language to the country in which it is spoken.

Write the letter of the correct language on each line.

א. טוּרְקִית	1. בְּיִשְׂרָאֵל הַשָׂפָה _____
ב. גֶּרְמָנִית	2. בְּרוּסְיָה הַשָׂפָה _____
ג. עִבְרִית	3. בְּפּוֹלִין הַשָׂפָה _____
ד. אִיטַלְקִית	4. בְּגֶרְמַנְיָה הַשָׂפָה _____
ה. פּוֹלָנִית	5. בְּטוּרְקִיָה הַשָׂפָה _____
ו. רוסית	6. בְּאִיטַלְיָה הַשָׂפָה _____

הַשָּׂפוֹת שֶׁל עַם יִשְׂרָאֵל

Rebecca spent the summer with her grandparents. Grandma Mizrachi came to America from Italy and Grandpa Mizrachi came from Turkey. Both of them are Sephardic. In addition to speaking the languages of the countries where they grew up, they both speak Ladino. Ladino is a Sephardic Jewish language that developed from Spanish.

Isaac went to Europe with his grandparents. He was very surprised to discover that they could speak several languages. Grandma Klein grew up in Poland. Grandpa Klein was born in Russia, but moved to Germany as a boy. Both of them also speak Yiddish. Yiddish is an Ashkenazic Jewish language that developed from German.

All four grandparents studied Hebrew when they were young. They use their Hebrew whenever they visit Israel and as the Jewish language of prayer.

Draw lines to connect the people to the languages they speak in addition to English.

Prayerobics

Because praying the עֲמִידָה is like appearing before God's royal court, many congregations use a special procedure at the beginning of the עֲמִידָה. Here's how it works.

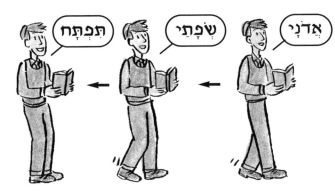

אֲדֹנָי שְׂפָתַי תִּפְתָּח

1. Begin with the left foot. On each of the first three words, take a small step backwards. On the last word, put your feet together.

וּפִי יַגִּיד תְּהִלָּתֶךָ

2. Begin with the right foot. Take a small step forward on each of the last three words.

Personal Prayer Parchment

When we recite the עֲמִידָה, the direction we face is important. Maimonides explains:

> *How do we face the (ancient) Temple? If you are outside of Israel, you face Israel. If you are in Israel, you face toward Jerusalem; in Jerusalem you face toward the Temple Mount. If you are in the Temple, you face the Holy of Holies. A blind person, or one who cannot find the proper direction, or one who is on a ship, should concentrate on God's presence and pray.* (Maimonides, Hilchot Tefillot 5:3)

Imagine that your prayer is being sent express to Jerusalem as you recite the opening line of the עֲמִידָה quietly to yourself.

אֲדֹנָי שְׂפָתַי תִּפְתָּח וּפִי יַגִּיד תְּהִלָּתֶךָ

As you stand in God's royal court, it's time to introduce yourself by reminding God of who you are and who your family is.

CHAPTER 1

"Our God Is the God of Our Ancestors."

דַּף קְרִיאָה
READING PAGE

KEY WORD:
אָבוֹת

In each line below, cross out the word that does not belong.

כַּרְפַּס	פֶּסַח	קִדּוּשׁ	אָלֶף	הַגָּדָה	מַצָּה	1.
שִׂמְחָה	פִּלְפֵּל	יַיִן	קָפֶה	חַלָּה	סָלָט	2.
אֶסְתֵּר	רִבְקָה	שָׂרָה	מִצְוָה	לֵאָה	רָחֵל	3.
דָוִד	עֶרֶב	יִצְחָק	אַבְרָהָם	דָּנִיֵּאל	אָדָם	4.
עֶשֶׂר	נֵר	חֲנֻכִּיָּה	לוּלָב	סֻכָּה	פּוּרִים	5.
הַפְטָרָה	חַזָּן	טַלִּית	סִדּוּר	סוֹף	בַּת-מִצְוָה	6.
מָגֵן דָּוִד	זָהָב	חֵיפָה	תֵּל אָבִיב	עִבְרִית	יִשְׂרָאֵל	7.

SUPER READING SECRET

Super readers combine syllables into whole words, and single words into fluent phrases.

Practice reading these prayer words and phrases.

ל + בְּנֵי = לִבְנֵי

לִבְנֵי + בְּנֵיהֶם = לִבְנֵי בְנֵיהֶם

עֶל + יוֹן = עֶלְיוֹן   וָא + ל + הֵי = וֵאלֹהֵי   יִצְ + חָק = יִצְחָק

אֵל + עֶלְיוֹן = אֵל עֶלְיוֹן   וֵאלֹהֵי + יַעֲקֹב = וֵאלֹהֵי יַעֲקֹב

אֱלֹהֵי + יִצְחָק = אֱלֹהֵי יִצְחָק

אֱלֹהֵינוּ וֵאלֹהֵי אֲבוֹתֵינוּ וְאִמּוֹתֵינוּ   מֶלֶךְ עוֹזֵר וּמוֹשִׁיעַ   הַגָּדוֹל הַגִּבּוֹר וְהַנּוֹרָא

The אָבוֹת prayer describes God as being the shield of our ancestors — our אָבוֹת וְאִמָּהוֹת.

The Twelve Gates

> There are twelve gates through which the prayers of Israel ascend into heaven. Each tradition has its own gate. Thus, each Israelite should pray according to his or her own tradition so as not to bring confusion into the higher realms. (Rabbi Isaac Luria, 1534 - 1572)

Traditional Version

Blessed is the Eternal	1. בָּרוּךְ אַתָּה יְיָ,
our God and God of our fathers.	2. אֱלֹהֵינוּ וֵאלֹהֵי אֲבוֹתֵינוּ:
The God of Abraham,	3. אֱלֹהֵי אַבְרָהָם,
the God of Isaac,	4. אֱלֹהֵי יִצְחָק,
and the God of Jacob.	5. וֵאלֹהֵי יַעֲקֹב.
Great, mighty and awesome God,	6. הָאֵל הַגָּדוֹל הַגִּבּוֹר וְהַנּוֹרָא,
God supreme.	7. אֵל עֶלְיוֹן.
You do great kindness and own everything	8. גּוֹמֵל חֲסָדִים טוֹבִים, וְקוֹנֵה הַכֹּל
and remember the kind deeds of our fathers	9. וְזוֹכֵר חַסְדֵי אָבוֹת
and bring a Redeemer	10. וּמֵבִיא גוֹאֵל
to their children's children	11. לִבְנֵי בְנֵיהֶם
for the sake of Your Name.	12. לְמַעַן שְׁמוֹ, בְּאַהֲבָה.
Ruler, Helper, Rescuer, and Shield,	13. מֶלֶךְ עוֹזֵר וּמוֹשִׁיעַ וּמָגֵן.
Blessed are You, Adonai,	14. בָּרוּךְ אַתָּה יְיָ,
the Shield of Abraham.	15. מָגֵן אַבְרָהָם.

☐ = in Traditional version

When the אָבוֹת was written, Jews believed that a military leader called מָשִׁיחַ would free them from oppression. Over time people began to think of the מָשִׁיחַ as a mystical redeemer who would raise the righteous from the dead, bring the Jewish people to the land of Israel, and establish world peace.

The early Reform Rabbis changed this idea. They prayed for a time of world peace, a "Messianic Age." They substituted the phrase וּמֵבִיא גְאֻלָּה ("brings redemption") for וּמֵבִיא גוֹאֵל ("brings a מָשִׁיחַ"). It is important to note that Jewish communities have always had a hopeful and optimistic view of the future.

Describe your vision of the future.

Blessed is the Eternal	בָּרוּךְ אַתָּה יְיָ,	.1
our God and God of our fathers *and mothers*.	אֱלֹהֵינוּ וֵאלֹהֵי אֲבוֹתֵינוּ וְאִמּוֹתֵינוּ:	.2
The God of Abraham,	אֱלֹהֵי אַבְרָהָם,	.3
the God of Isaac	אֱלֹהֵי יִצְחָק,	.4
and the God of Jacob.	וֵאלֹהֵי יַעֲקֹב:	.5
The God of Sarah,	אֱלֹהֵי שָׂרָה,	5א.
the God of Rebecca,	אֱלֹהֵי רִבְקָה,	5ב.
the God of Leah, and the God of Rachel.	אֱלֹהֵי לֵאָה, וֵאלֹהֵי רָחֵל.	5ג.
Great, mighty, and awesome God,	הָאֵל הַגָּדוֹל הַגִּבּוֹר וְהַנּוֹרָא,	.6
God supreme.	אֵל עֶלְיוֹן.	.7
You do great kindness and own everything	גּוֹמֵל חֲסָדִים טוֹבִים, וְקוֹנֵה הַכֹּל,	.8
and remember the kind deeds of our fathers *and mothers*	וְזוֹכֵר חַסְדֵי אָבוֹת וְאִמָּהוֹת,	.9
and bring *Redemption*	וּמֵבִיא גְאֻלָּה	.10
to their children's children	לִבְנֵי בְנֵיהֶם,	.11
for the sake of Your Name.	לְמַעַן שְׁמוֹ, בְּאַהֲבָה.	.12
Ruler, Helper, Rescuer, and Shield,	מֶלֶךְ עוֹזֵר וּמוֹשִׁיעַ וּמָגֵן.	.13
Blessed are You, Adonai,	בָּרוּךְ אַתָּה יְיָ,	.14
the Shield of Abraham *and Help of Sarah*.	מָגֵן אַבְרָהָם וְעֶזְרַת שָׂרָה.	.15

= in some Liberal versions

Understanding the Prayer Differences

אָבוֹת וְאִמָּהוֹת

Check each statement with which you agree.

Reasons to add the אִמָּהוֹת

❏ Modern people recognize that men and women are equal. We need to acknowledge our mothers, too.

❏ The contributions of women have often been ignored. Both boys and girls need to learn about the contributions of great women in Jewish history.

❏ Our prayers should be meaningful for our times. The words of many prayers have been changed in the past.

Reasons not to add the אִמָּהוֹת

❏ God made direct promises to all of the fathers, but only to one of the mothers.

❏ Traditional Judaism recognizes that men and women are different, and recognizes the value of women in different ways. The Rabbis told many stories about the good works and characters of women.

❏ It's important for all Jews to use the same words during prayer. It keeps us together as a people.

הַמִּשְׁפָּחָה שֶׁל רִבְקָה

אוֹצָר מִלִּים
A TREASURY OF WORDS

I have = יֵשׁ לִי

Fill in the blanks to complete the information about Rebecca's family.

אֲנִי אָב.
יֵשׁ לִי בֵּן.
יֵשׁ לִי _____.

אֲנִי אֵם.
יֵשׁ לִי בֵּן.
יֵשׁ לִי בַּת.

אֲנִי בַּת.
יֵשׁ לִי _____.
_____ אֵם.
_____ _____.

אֲנִי בֵּן.
_____ אָב.
יֵשׁ לִי _____.
_____ אָחוֹת.

Now look at the foundation of every Jewish family.

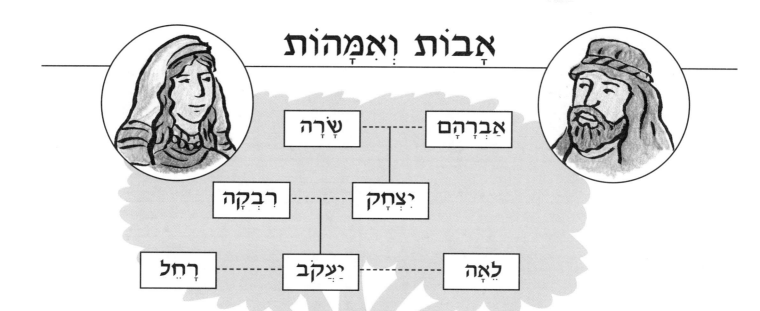

אָבוֹת וְאִמָּהוֹת

Family tree:

שָׂרָה — אַבְרָהָם

רִבְקָה — יִצְחָק

רָחֵל — יַעֲקֹב — לֵאָה

Study the family tree of our אָבוֹת וְאִמָּהוֹת, **then complete the crossword puzzle. Do not use vowels.**

Across	Down
2. הָאָב שֶׁל יִצְחָק.	1. הָאָחוֹת שֶׁל רָחֵל.
4. הָאֵם שֶׁל יִצְחָק.	3. הָאָחוֹת שֶׁל לֵאָה.
6. הַבֵּן שֶׁל אַבְרָהָם וְשָׂרָה.	5. הָאֵם שֶׁל יַעֲקֹב.
	6. הַבֵּן שֶׁל יִצְחָק וְרִבְקָה.

In the אָבוֹת prayer, we introduce ourselves to God by reminding God about our family.

Family Ties

A few minutes before the start of Hebrew school, the students began to gather in Mrs. Shapiro's classroom. Many of them had not seen each other over the summer vacation, and were now busy catching up. Rebecca told Mrs. Shapiro about her summer in New York, and Isaac showed everyone his pictures from Europe. Yossi, Michael, and Danny talked about their soccer league, and Sarah showed off her swimming medal from Jewish summer camp.

As the bell rang, Esther bounced in with a new student. "Hi, Mrs. Shapiro. This is Ilana Kaplan. She just moved in next door to me," Esther announced.

"Welcome to our class, Ilana," Mrs. Shapiro said as the students found their seats. "Why don't you tell us about yourself."

"Well, I like tennis, and I was in a really cool acting group this summer. We did *Fiddler on the Roof*, and I got to play Tzeitel."

"Where are you from?" Danny asked.

"Washington, but my parents are from here. We moved back to be near my grandparents."

Mrs. Shapiro looked at Ilana for a moment. "Kaplan? Are your parents Miriam and Ben Kaplan?"

Ilana nodded. "Yeah, they're my parents."

Mrs. Shapiro burst out laughing. "Well, that's unbelievable! I taught both of your parents. I know your grandparents, too. I had no idea your family was moving back."

Yossi gasped. "You mean you've been teaching Hebrew school that long?"

"Yes, Yossi," Mrs. Shapiro replied. "Since the Ice Age. In fact, I even had *your* parents in class, and they were great students."

How would you feel if your parents and grandparents had a personal connection to your teacher?

❑ Oh, no! Now I'll have to live up to their standards.

❑ I'm my own person. My teacher won't judge me because of them.

❑ Cool. Maybe my teacher will give me special treatment because she knows them.

הַמִּשְׁפָּחָה שֶׁל אִילָנָה

סַבְתָּא   סַבָּא   סַבְתָּא   סַבָּא

דּוֹד מֹשֶׁה   אִמָּא   אַבָּא   דּוֹדָה חַנָה

דָּוִד   אִילָנָה   רָחֵל

Find the Relationships

Study the chart of Ilana's family tree. Then fill in the missing words

below to make the relationships correct.

1. דָּוִד הוּא הַ_____ שֶׁל אִילָנָה.

2. רָחֵל הִיא הַ_____ שֶׁל דָּוִד.

3. דּוֹד מֹשֶׁה הוּא הָאָח שֶׁל _____.

4. דּוֹדָה חַנָה הִיא הָאָחוֹת שֶׁל _____.

5. הָאַבָּא שֶׁל אִמָּא הוּא הַ_____ שֶׁל אִילָנָה.

6. הַסַּבְתָּא שֶׁל אִילָנָה הִיא הַ_____ שֶׁל אַבָּא.

Prayerobics

In the opening line of the עֲמִידָה, you formally approached the royal court. (You can find the steps on page 8.) Here are the next steps.

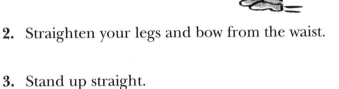

1. Bend your knees.

2. Straighten your legs and bow from the waist.

3. Stand up straight.

4. These three movements are repeated when reciting the closing blessing of the אָבוֹת.

5. During all of the עֲמִידָה, some people rock or sway rhythmically. In Yiddish, this is called *shuckeling*, and it can help us feel the power of the עֲמִידָה as we say it.

Practice reciting the אָבוֹת with these special movements.

Where We Stand

Put a check next to each sentence that is illustrated in a picture above.

☐ 1. דָּנִיֵּאל עוֹמֵד עִם סִדּוּר.

☐ 2. דָּנִיֵּאל אוֹכֵל לֶחֶם.

☐ 3. שָׂרָה עוֹמֶדֶת עַל-יַד סַבְתָּא.

☐ 4. שָׂרָה עוֹמֶדֶת בְּבֵית-הַכְּנֶסֶת.

☐ 5. דָּנִיֵּאל עוֹמֵד עַל-יַד הַשֻּׁלְחָן.

☐ 6. שָׂרָה אוֹהֶבֶת אֶת הַכֶּלֶב.

עוֹמֶדֶת   עוֹמֵד

Personal Prayer Parchment

KEY WORD: אָבוֹת

Having introduced yourself in God's royal court, take a minute to record your thoughts about the opening blessing of the עֲמִידָה.

1. List three things that make you proud of your family.

_____   _____

2. What makes your family proud of you?

_____

3. What would you like God to know about you and your family?

_____

Keep these thoughts in your heart as you recite the אָבוֹת *quietly to yourself.*

Traditional Version

בָּרוּךְ אַתָּה יְיָ, אֱלֹהֵינוּ וֵאלֹהֵי אֲבוֹתֵינוּ: אֱלֹהֵי אַבְרָהָם, אֱלֹהֵי יִצְחָק,

וֵאלֹהֵי יַעֲקֹב. הָאֵל הַגָּדוֹל הַגִּבּוֹר וְהַנּוֹרָא, אֵל עֶלְיוֹן. גּוֹמֵל חֲסָדִים

טוֹבִים, וְקוֹנֵה הַכֹּל, וְזוֹכֵר חַסְדֵי אָבוֹת, וּמֵבִיא גוֹאֵל לִבְנֵי בְנֵיהֶם,

לְמַעַן שְׁמוֹ, בְּאַהֲבָה. מֶלֶךְ עוֹזֵר וּמוֹשִׁיעַ וּמָגֵן. בָּרוּךְ אַתָּה יְיָ, מָגֵן אַבְרָהָם.

A Liberal Version

בָּרוּךְ אַתָּה יְיָ, אֱלֹהֵינוּ וֵאלֹהֵי אֲבוֹתֵינוּ וְאִמּוֹתֵינוּ: אֱלֹהֵי אַבְרָהָם,

אֱלֹהֵי יִצְחָק, וֵאלֹהֵי יַעֲקֹב, אֱלֹהֵי שָׂרָה, אֱלֹהֵי רִבְקָה, אֱלֹהֵי

לֵאָה, וֵאלֹהֵי רָחֵל. הָאֵל הַגָּדוֹל הַגִּבּוֹר וְהַנּוֹרָא, אֵל עֶלְיוֹן.

גּוֹמֵל חֲסָדִים טוֹבִים, וְקוֹנֵה הַכֹּל, וְזוֹכֵר חַסְדֵי אָבוֹת וְאִמָּהוֹת,

וּמֵבִיא גְאֻלָּה לִבְנֵי בְנֵיהֶם, לְמַעַן שְׁמוֹ, בְּאַהֲבָה. מֶלֶךְ עוֹזֵר

וּמוֹשִׁיעַ וּמָגֵן. בָּרוּךְ אַתָּה יְיָ, מָגֵן אַבְרָהָם וְעֶזְרַת שָׂרָה.

After introducing yourself to God, it's time to show your respect for God's awesome power.

CHAPTER 2

"Our God Is a Hero Who Works Miraculous Rescues."

גְּבוּרוֹת

דַּף קְרִיאָה
READING PAGE

KEY WORD:
גִבּוֹר

Two of the words below are the names of Jewish biblical heroes. Circle them.

הַגִּבּוֹר	עֶלְיוֹן	שָׁלוֹם	גּוֹאֵל	עוֹזֵר	סוֹפֵר	סוֹף	1.
בֹּקֶר טוֹב	חָמֵץ	טִבְעוֹנִי	יַעֲקֹב	וָרֶד	הַכֹּל	בֹּקֶר	2.
מִי כָמוֹךְ	בְּחֶסֶד	הַגֶּשֶׁם	דּוֹמֶה	אֱלֹהֵינוּ	בַּעַל	מֶלֶךְ	3.
חַג שָׂמֵחַ	הָאָרֶץ	לְהוֹשִׁיעַ	וּמַצְמִיחַ	כֹּחַ	הָרוּחַ	לוּחַ	4.
בֵּית-כְּנֶסֶת	מְחַיֵּה	זְכוּת	גְּבוּרוֹת	סְלִיחָה	בְּבַקָּשָׁה	בְּרָכָה	5.
מְכַלְכֵּל	בְּרַחֲמִים	וְנֶאֱמָן	לְהַחֲיוֹת	יְשׁוּעָה	וְרוֹפֵא	לְחַיִּים	6.
תְּהִלָּתֶךָ	אֱלֹהֶיךָ	אֱלֹהֶיךָ	נְבִיאֶךָ	וְתִמְלוֹךְ	בַּדֶּרֶךְ	לָךְ	7.
עֵץ חַיִּים	יִצְחָק	אֲדֹנָי	אֲדֹנָי	שְׂפָתַי	חַיִּים	חַי	8.

SUPER READING SECRET

Super readers blend single words into smooth phrases. Practice blending these phrases.

מְכַלְכֵּל חַיִּים בְּחֶסֶד	מְכַלְכֵּל + חַיִּים + בְּחֶסֶד	1.
וְנֶאֱמָן אַתָּה לְהַחֲיוֹת מֵתִים	וְנֶאֱמָן + אַתָּה + לְהַחֲיוֹת + מֵתִים	2.
וְנֶאֱמָן אַתָּה לְהַחֲיוֹת הַכֹּל	וְנֶאֱמָן + אַתָּה + לְהַחֲיוֹת + הַכֹּל	3.
וּמְקַיֵּם אֱמוּנָתוֹ לִישֵׁנֵי עָפָר	וּמְקַיֵּם + אֱמוּנָתוֹ + לִישֵׁנֵי + עָפָר	4.
מֶלֶךְ מֵמִית וּמְחַיֶּה וּמַצְמִיחַ יְשׁוּעָה	מֶלֶךְ + מֵמִית + וּמְחַיֶּה + וּמַצְמִיחַ + יְשׁוּעָה	5.

Rescue at Entebbe

In the early hours of July 4, 1976, a miraculous rescue took place. Eight days earlier, terrorists had hijacked a French airplane after it left Tel Aviv, and ordered the pilot to fly to the Entebbe Airport in the African country of Uganda.

The hijackers threatened to kill the hostages unless Israel released several convicted terrorists. Jewish passengers were separated from the rest of the group, reminding many of the terrible "selections" that took place during the Holocaust. After three days, all of the non-Jewish passengers were released, and the hijackers set a deadline. If their demands were not met by July 4th at 11:00 A.M., they would begin to kill the hostages.

On the night of July 3rd, fear and tension filled the hot, stuffy room where the hostages were held. Two of the hostages, Uzi and Sara Davidson, kept diaries to pass the long hours of captivity. Here is Uzi Davidson's account of what happened that night:

From outside I heard two or three bursts of fire. Then another single bullet. I raised my head, and I saw the hijackers jump from their places. We were at the edge of the hall. I had no idea what was happening. I thought one of the Ugandan soldiers had accidentally fired his gun. I feared there was going to be trouble.

I lost any sense of time, but I think that within two seconds I had the family crawling toward the toilet. There was a wall there where we could take cover. I don't know how long we lay there. It must have been minutes. It seemed like five years going on and on.

Outside, there was a serious clash in progress, with shooting and explosions. We did not exchange a word. I did not see the terrorists.

Somebody in the hall straightened up and called, "Yes, yes, Israeli soldiers, Israeli soldiers," and while I was still wondering why the man was shouting such nonsense, I saw one of the most wonderful sights I have ever seen. Next to us stood an Israeli soldier of Yemenite extraction— short, thin, carrying a Kalachnikov rifle two sizes too large for him. He was as cool as though he had dropped by to invite us for a drink, just by chance. He said, "Shalom, fellows. Everything is all right. Get up calmly, and come with me. We're taking you home."

This daring rescue was given the code name "Operation Thunderbolt." It lasted only 90 minutes. Four large Israeli transport planes slipped quietly onto the back runways of Entebbe's airport. As the planes touched down, a light rain began to fall. The night, fog, and drizzle provided cover for the teams of Israeli commandos as they raced to save the hostages.

CHAPTER **2**

It all happened very fast. One team of commandos shot the terrorist guards, and a second team took the Ugandan soldiers by surprise. Before the terrorists inside the lounge could get out the door, two teams of Israeli commandos burst into the lounge to meet them. The shooting inside lasted less than two minutes, and quickly the hostages were led to the safety of the transport planes.

Sara Davidson's last entry says it best:

There is a verse: "God's redemption comes like the twinkling of an eye." When we heard the sudden shooting, I repeated the Sh'ma Yisrael! that a Jew says when the hour has come.
And a soldier leaped toward me with Hebrew on his tongue. I felt goose pimples. I would not die, but live to tell the deeds of God.

(Adapted from *90 Minutes at Entebbe* by William Stevenson. Bantam Books, Inc., New York, 1976)

TEXT EXploration

Hero = גִּבּוֹר

Heroine = גִּבּוֹרָה

hero (hîr-ō) (mas.)/**heroine** (hĕr´ō-ĭn) (fem.), n.,

1. In mythology and legend, a human being endowed with superhuman strength, who is celebrated for bold exploits.
2. A person noted for feats of courage or nobility of purpose, especially one who has risked or sacrificed his or her life.
3. A person noted for special achievement in a particular field.
4. The principal character in a novel, poem, or dramatic presentation.

The phrases below come from the גְּבוּרוֹת prayer. In the space provided, write the number of the definition that best describes each of God's heroic acts. Then use the list of the heroic things God does to create a precise definition of what a גִּבּוֹרָה or גִּבּוֹר should do.

____ You sustain the living with kindness   מְכַלְכֵּל חַיִּים בְּחֶסֶד

____ You lift up the fallen   סוֹמֵךְ נוֹפְלִים

____ You heal the sick   רוֹפֵא חוֹלִים

____ You set the captives free   מַתִּיר אֲסוּרִים

____ You keep faith with those who sleep in the dust   מְקַיֵּם אֱמוּנָתוֹ לִישֵׁנֵי עָפָר

A גִּבּוֹר is: _____

גִּבּוֹרֵי יִשְׂרָאֵל

**On the line below each person's description,
copy the Hebrew phrase that you think best describes his or her heroic actions.**

רוֹפֵא חוֹלִים   סוֹמֵךְ נוֹפְלִים

מְקַיֵּם אֱמוּנָתוֹ לִישֵׁנֵי עָפָר   מַתִּיר אֲסוּרִים

חַנָּה סֶנֶשׁ

During World War II, this poet and "woman of valor" parachuted behind Nazi lines in an effort to rescue the Jews in Hungary. Captured and executed by the Nazis, she never betrayed her comrades.

מֹשֶׁה דַּיָּן

He was one of Israel's greatest military leaders, known for his courage and intelligence during war. His efforts to rescue his wounded men and to recover the bodies of Israel's soldiers who had fallen in battle were exceptional.

יִצְחָק רַבִּין

He was a fierce warrior. Yet he will best be remembered as the Prime Minister who set out on a quest for peace. Before he was assassinated, his efforts brought hope and dignity to both the Israelis and the Palestinians.

הֶנְרִיאֶטָה סוֹלְד

This great American philanthropist raised money for people in trouble around the globe. She is best known for founding Hadassah Hospital so that the poor of Jerusalem could have access to quality medical care.

גּוֹלְדָה מֵאִיר

She was Israel's first woman Prime Minister. She called for the release of the Jews in the former Soviet Union, who were engaged in an open struggle for the right to settle in Israel.

יוֹנִי נְתַנְיָהוּ

He was the Commander of the elite commando unit that rescued the Israeli hostages at Entebbe and was the only Israeli soldier killed during this operation. His brother, Benjamin, became Prime Minister of Israel.

Based on what you have learned, who do you think of as a גִּבּוֹר or גְּבוֹרָה?

In the גְּבוּרוֹת prayer, God is described as a גִּבּוֹר.

The Twelve Gates

> There are twelve gates through which the prayers of Israel ascend into heaven. Each tradition has its own gate. Thus, each Israelite should pray according to his or her own tradition so as not to bring confusion into the higher realms.
>
> (Rabbi Isaac Luria, 1534 - 1572)

Traditional Version

You are mighty forever, Adonai,	1. אַתָּה גִבּוֹר לְעוֹלָם, אֲדֹנָי,
You give life to the dead,	2. מְחַיֵּה מֵתִים אַתָּה,
You are a great Rescuer.	3. רַב לְהוֹשִׁיעַ.
You sustain the living with kindness,	4. מְכַלְכֵּל חַיִּים בְּחֶסֶד,
You give life to the dead	5. מְחַיֵּה מֵתִים
with great compassion.	6. בְּרַחֲמִים רַבִּים.
You lift up the fallen, and heal the sick,	7. סוֹמֵךְ נוֹפְלִים, וְרוֹפֵא חוֹלִים,
and set the captives free,	8. וּמַתִּיר אֲסוּרִים,
and keep faith with those who sleep in the dust.	9. וּמְקַיֵּם אֱמוּנָתוֹ לִישֵׁנֵי עָפָר.
Who is like You, Sovereign of might,	10. מִי כָמוֹךָ בַּעַל גְּבוּרוֹת, וּמִי דּוֹמֶה לָךְ,
Monarch, Life-giver, Source of Liberation?	11. מֶלֶךְ מֵמִית וּמְחַיֶּה וּמַצְמִיחַ יְשׁוּעָה?
Faithful are You to give life to the dead.	12. וְנֶאֱמָן אַתָּה לְהַחֲיוֹת מֵתִים.
Blessed are You, Adonai, You give life to the dead.	13. בָּרוּךְ אַתָּה יְיָ, מְחַיֵּה הַמֵּתִים.

☐ = Traditional version

Liberal Version

You are mighty forever, Adonai,	אַתָּה גִבּוֹר לְעוֹלָם, אֲדֹנָי,	1.
You give life to everything,	מְחַיֵּה הַכֹּל אַתָּה,	2.
You are a great Rescuer.	רַב לְהוֹשִׁיעַ.	3.
You sustain the living with kindness,	מְכַלְכֵּל חַיִּים בְּחֶסֶד,	4.
You give life to everything	מְחַיֵּה הַכֹּל	5.
with great compassion.	בְּרַחֲמִים רַבִּים.	6.
You lift up the fallen, and heal the sick,	סוֹמֵךְ נוֹפְלִים, וְרוֹפֵא חוֹלִים,	7.
and set the captives free.	וּמַתִּיר אֲסוּרִים,	8.
and keep faith with those who sleep in the dust.	וּמְקַיֵּם אֱמוּנָתוֹ לִישֵׁנֵי עָפָר.	9.
Who is like You, Sovereign of might,	מִי כָמוֹךָ בַּעַל גְּבוּרוֹת, וּמִי דּוֹמֶה לָּךְ,	10.
Monarch, Life-giver, Source of Liberation?	מֶלֶךְ מֵמִית וּמְחַיֶּה וּמַצְמִיחַ יְשׁוּעָה?	11.
Faithful are You to give life to everything.	וְנֶאֱמָן אַתָּה לְהַחֲיוֹת הַכֹּל.	12.
Blessed are You, Adonai, You give life to everything.	בָּרוּךְ אַתָּה יְיָ, מְחַיֵּה הַכֹּל.	13.

= Liberal version

Understanding the Prayer Differences

the dead = מֵתִים   everything = הַכֹּל

What happens after we die? People have asked this question throughout history. No one really knows the answer, but over the centuries, many different beliefs have developed. When the גְּבוּרוֹת was written, most Jews believed that the dead would be brought back to life when the Messiah arrived. Early Reform Rabbis did not believe in resurrection. They substituted the word הַכֹּל for מֵתִים to express the idea that God is the source of all life.

Check each answer that you believe now, or have believed at some time.

❑ Death is the end of one's existence.
❑ At some time, the righteous dead will be brought back to life.
❑ After death, the spirit is reborn in a new body, either human or animal.
❑ We are bound up in a cycle of life. Our bodies decompose, enriching the earth.
❑ After death, we live on in the memory of those who love us.

The גְּבוּרוֹת prayer describes God as a רוֹפֵא חוֹלִים (healer of the sick).
Now learn some Hebrew words about the healing that people can do.

אוֹצַר מִלִים
A TREASURY OF WORDS

Possessive Pronouns

my or mine = שֶׁלִי

yours (masc. sing.) = שֶׁלְךָ

yours (fem. sing.) = שֶׁלָךְ

his = שֶׁלוֹ

hers = שֶׁלָה

בֵּית-חוֹלִים

חוֹלָה

חוֹלֶה

רוֹפְאָה

רוֹפֵא

Fill in each blank with the correct possessive pronoun from page 24.

הַכֶּלֶב _____ .

הַצִּפּוֹר _____ .

הוּא הַבֵּן _____ .

הִיא הַדּוֹדָה _____ .

מִי הָרוֹפְאָה _____ ?

הִיא הַסַּבְתָּא _____ ?

הִיא הָרוֹפְאָה _____ .

כֵּן, הִיא הַסַּבְתָּא שֶׁלִּי.

מִי בַּכִּתָּה?

הַמּוֹרָה: שָׁלוֹם יוֹסִי.

יוֹסִי: שָׁלוֹם הַמּוֹרָה שַׁפִּירוֹ.

הַמּוֹרָה: אֵיפֹה כָּל הַתַּלְמִידִים?

יוֹסִי: אֵין תַּלְמִידִים בַּכִּתָּה הַיּוֹם.

הַמּוֹרָה: אֵיפֹה רִבְקָה?

יוֹסִי: הִיא בַּבַּיִת שֶׁל הַדּוֹדָה שֶׁלָּה.

הַמּוֹרָה: אֵיפֹה שָׂרָה?

יוֹסִי: הִיא בְּבֵית-חוֹלִים. הַסַּבָּא שֶׁלָּה חוֹלֶה.

הַמּוֹרָה: אֵיפֹה דָּנִיֵּאל?

יוֹסִי: הוּא בְּתֵל אָבִיב.

הַמּוֹרָה: אֵיפֹה יִצְחָק?

יוֹסִי: יִצְחָק חוֹלֶה. הוּא רוֹאֶה אֶת הָרוֹפֵא שֶׁלּוֹ.

הַמּוֹרָה: אֵיפֹה אֶסְתֵּר?

יוֹסִי: בַּכִּתָּה שֶׁל הָאָחוֹת שֶׁלָּה.

הַמּוֹרָה: אֵיפֹה אִילָנָה?

יוֹסִי: הִיא בַּבַּיִת. הִיא חוֹלָה.

הַמּוֹרָה: אוֹי...

יוֹסִי: אַתְּ רוֹאָה, אֵין תַּלְמִידִים בַּכִּתָּה הַיּוֹם

הַמּוֹרָה: אַתָּה תַּלְמִיד, יוֹסִי, וְאַתָּה בַּכִּתָּה הַיּוֹם!

1. מִי בְּאֶרֶץ יִשְׂרָאֵל? _____

2. מִי בַּבַּיִת שֶׁל הַדּוֹדָה? _____ .

3. מִי בְּבֵית-חוֹלִים? _____ .

4. מִי חוֹלֶה? _____ וְ _____ .

5. מִי חוֹלָה? _____ .

6. מִי בַּכִּתָּה? _____ וְ _____ .

Personal Prayer Parchment

The גְּבוּרוֹת teaches us that God works miraculous rescues. It also reminds us that God is a hero, and that we should strive to become like God. Take a minute now to record your thoughts about the second blessing of the עֲמִידָה.

How does it feel:

1. To be saved from something at the last minute?

   _____

2. When someone treats you kindly?

   _____

3. If someone "lifts you up" when you're feeling low?

   _____

Keep these thoughts in your heart while you recite the גְּבוּרוֹת quietly to yourself.

Traditional Version

אַתָּה גִּבּוֹר לְעוֹלָם, אֲדֹנָי, מְחַיֵּה מֵתִים אַתָּה, רַב לְהוֹשִׁיעַ. מְכַלְכֵּל חַיִּים בְּחֶסֶד,
מְחַיֵּה מֵתִים בְּרַחֲמִים רַבִּים. סוֹמֵךְ נוֹפְלִים, וְרוֹפֵא חוֹלִים, וּמַתִּיר אֲסוּרִים,
וּמְקַיֵּם אֱמוּנָתוֹ לִישֵׁנֵי עָפָר. מִי כָמוֹךָ בַּעַל גְּבוּרוֹת, וּמִי דּוֹמֶה לָּךְ, מֶלֶךְ מֵמִית
וּמְחַיֵּה וּמַצְמִיחַ יְשׁוּעָה? וְנֶאֱמָן אַתָּה לְהַחֲיוֹת מֵתִים. בָּרוּךְ אַתָּה יְיָ, מְחַיֵּה הַמֵּתִים.

Liberal Version

אַתָּה גִּבּוֹר לְעוֹלָם, אֲדֹנָי, מְחַיֵּה הַכֹּל אַתָּה, רַב לְהוֹשִׁיעַ. מְכַלְכֵּל חַיִּים בְּחֶסֶד,
מְחַיֵּה הַכֹּל בְּרַחֲמִים רַבִּים. סוֹמֵךְ נוֹפְלִים, וְרוֹפֵא חוֹלִים, וּמַתִּיר אֲסוּרִים,
וּמְקַיֵּם אֱמוּנָתוֹ לִישֵׁנֵי עָפָר. מִי כָמוֹךָ בַּעַל גְּבוּרוֹת, וּמִי דּוֹמֶה לָּךְ, מֶלֶךְ מֵמִית
וּמְחַיֵּה וּמַצְמִיחַ יְשׁוּעָה? וְנֶאֱמָן אַתָּה לְהַחֲיוֹת הַכֹּל. בָּרוּךְ אַתָּה יְיָ, מְחַיֵּה הַכֹּל.

Now that you've learned about God's powers, and how you can use your own powers to improve the world, it's time to explore the question of just how unique God really is.

CHAPTER 3

"Our God Is Unique in All the World."

קְדֻשָּׁה

דַּף קְרִיאָה
READING PAGE

KEY WORD:
קָדוֹשׁ

SUPER READING SECRET

How is ָ pronounced when it is followed by a silent ְ ? _____

Practice reading these words.

גָּדְלוּ   בְּגָבְהֵי   זָכְרֵנוּ

Practice reading these words and phrases.

1. כָּל   בְּכָל   חָכְמָה   חָפְשִׁי   קִדְּשׁוֹ   קִדַּשְׁךָ   גָּדְלֶךָ   וּבְשָׁכְבְּךָ

2. הִנְנִי   עֲנֵנִי   רוֹמְמוּ   הַלְלוּ   יְהַלְלוּ   הַלְלוּיָה   יְהַלְלוּךָ   וּנְרוֹמְמָה

3. שָׂמֵחַ   לוּחַ   רוּחַ   סוֹלֵחַ   כֹּחַ   לִזְרוֹחַ   שָׁלִיחַ   מָשִׁיחַ

4. קֹדֶשׁ   נְקַדֵּשׁ   קָדוֹשׁ   מְקַדֵּשׁ   קִדְּשׁוֹ   קַדִּישׁ   קָדְשׁוֹ   קָדְשֶׁךָ   קָדְשְׁךָ

5. לְדוֹר וָדוֹר נַגִּיד גָּדְלֶךָ

6. אֱלֹהַיִךְ צִיּוֹן, לְדֹר וָדֹר. הַלְלוּיָה!

7. עַל-יְדֵי דָוִד מְשִׁיחַ צִדְקֶךָ:

8. וּקְדוֹשִׁים בְּכָל-יוֹם יְהַלְלוּךָ סֶּלָה.

9. מְלֹא כָל-הָאָרֶץ כְּבוֹדוֹ.

10. מָה-אַדִּיר שִׁמְךָ בְּכָל-הָאָרֶץ.

קִדּוּשִׁין

קִדּוּשׁ

בֵּית הַמִּקְדָּשׁ

אֲרוֹן הַקֹּדֶשׁ

The illustrated words all contain members of the ק.ד.שׁ. word family. Words from the ק.ד.שׁ. root mean "special," "set apart," "sacred," or "holy." Circle all the words on this page that contain the ק.ד.שׁ. root.

Praying Like the Angels

KEY WORD: קָדוֹשׁ

While the rest of the class was reading the קְדֻשָׁה with their partners, Danny and Isaac were quietly quizzing each other on their math review sheets. They were so busy with fractions that they didn't notice Mrs. Shapiro standing next to them.

"Okay, you two," Mrs. Shapiro said. "I know you have a big test tomorrow, but this is not the time to be doing your math."

Esther called from across the room, "If you guys don't know it by now, you're never going to get it!"

"Yeah, really," Yossi added. "You're better off just praying for it!"

"You're not supposed to pray for stuff like that, are you, Mrs. Shapiro?" Michael asked. "Shouldn't you just pray for big things like world peace?"

"Good question," Mrs. Shapiro answered. "What kind of prayers should we say?"

"I prayed that I'd get a good part in a play," Ilana said, "and I got it. I think it's okay to ask for the things you want."

"My grandpa said that it's not right to ask God for things we want," Rebecca said, "only for the things we need."

"I think there's something important that you're all missing here," Mrs. Shapiro said. "Do all of our prayers ask God for something?"

The class thought for a moment, then Esther said, "Well, the ones we've been studying this year sure don't."

Mrs. Shapiro smiled. "That's right. In fact, most of the prayers in our services don't ask for things. What do they do instead?"

"Mostly they just talk about how great God is," Yossi answered.

"Right again," Mrs. Shapiro said. "The three prayers we've been studying all praise God. In fact, the Rabbis taught that when we pray, we should pray like the angels. They never make requests. They only praise God."

Michael asked, "But what about asking God for things?"

"I'm going to hold off on your question, Michael. We'll discuss it in a couple of weeks when we get to the prayers that make requests of God. Meanwhile, think about the things that you'd praise God for doing. Your homework is to write the kind of prayer the angels might say."

Help the kids with their homework. Write your own prayer that praises God.

_____

_____

_____

Twelve Gates

We will sanctify Your Name in the world,	נְקַדֵּשׁ אֶת־שִׁמְךָ בָּעוֹלָם, 1.
as it is sanctified in the heavens above,	כְּשֵׁם שֶׁמַּקְדִּישִׁים אוֹתוֹ בִּשְׁמֵי מָרוֹם, 2.
as Your Prophet wrote:	כַּכָּתוּב עַל־יַד נְבִיאֶךָ: 3.
They called to one another saying:	וְקָרָא זֶה אֶל־זֶה וְאָמַר: 4.
Holy, holy, holy is Adonai of Hosts,	קָדוֹשׁ, קָדוֹשׁ, קָדוֹשׁ יְיָ צְבָאוֹת, 5.
the whole earth is filled with God's glory.	מְלֹא כָל־הָאָרֶץ כְּבוֹדוֹ. 6.
Powerful and mighty, our sovereign God,	אַדִּיר אַדִּירֵנוּ, יְיָ אֲדֹנֵינוּ, 6א.
How majestic is Your Name in all the earth.	מָה־אַדִּיר שִׁמְךָ בְּכָל־הָאָרֶץ. 6ב.
Blessed be the glory of God from its place.	בָּרוּךְ כְּבוֹד־יְיָ מִמְּקוֹמוֹ. 7.
Our God is One	אֶחָד הוּא אֱלֹהֵינוּ 7א.
God is our Parent, our Ruler, our Rescuer,	הוּא אָבִינוּ, הוּא מַלְכֵּנוּ, הוּא מוֹשִׁיעֵנוּ, 7ב.
and with compassion, God will rescue us	וְהוּא יַשְׁמִיעֵנוּ בְּרַחֲמָיו 7ג.
in the sight of all the living:	לְעֵינֵי כָּל־חָי: 7ד.
I am Adonai your God.	אֲנִי יְיָ אֱלֹהֵיכֶם. 7ה.
The Eternal One shall reign forever,	יִמְלֹךְ יְיָ לְעוֹלָם, 8.
Your God, O Zion,	אֱלֹהַיִךְ צִיּוֹן, 9.
from generation to generation. Halleluyah!	לְדֹר וָדֹר. הַלְלוּיָהּ! 10.
To all generations we will tell of Your greatness	לְדוֹר וָדוֹר נַגִּיד גָּדְלֶךָ 11.
and to all eternity we will sanctify Your sacredness.	וּלְנֵצַח נְצָחִים קְדֻשָּׁתְךָ נַקְדִּישׁ. 12.
Your praise, O God, will never depart	וְשִׁבְחֲךָ, אֱלֹהֵינוּ, מִפִּינוּ לֹא יָמוּשׁ 13.
from our lips.	לְעוֹלָם וָעֶד. 14.
Blessed are You Adonai, the Sacred God.	בָּרוּךְ אַתָּה יְיָ, הָאֵל הַקָּדוֹשׁ. 15.

= added in some Liberal versions

What ideas or images are only in the Traditional version?

We will sanctify Your Name in the world,	נְקַדֵּשׁ אֶת־שִׁמְךָ בָּעוֹלָם, 1.
as it is sanctified in the heavens above,	כְּשֵׁם שֶׁמַּקְדִּישִׁים אוֹתוֹ בִּשְׁמֵי מָרוֹם, 2.
as Your Prophet wrote:	כַּכָּתוּב עַל־יַד נְבִיאֶךָ: 3.
They called to one another saying:	וְקָרָא זֶה אֶל־זֶה וְאָמַר: 4.
Holy, holy, holy is Adonai of Hosts,	קָדוֹשׁ, קָדוֹשׁ, קָדוֹשׁ יְיָ צְבָאוֹת, 5.
the whole earth is filled with God's glory.	מְלֹא כָל־הָאָרֶץ כְּבוֹדוֹ. 6.

Then the angels, with one great loud voice	אָז בְּקוֹל רַעַשׁ גָּדוֹל 6א.
in a strong and mighty chorus	אַדִּיר וְחָזָק מַשְׁמִיעִים קוֹל 6ב.
rise up toward the seraphim	מִתְנַשְּׂאִים לְעֻמַּת שְׂרָפִים 6ג.
and respond with a blessing of their own:	לְעֻמָּתָם בָּרוּךְ יֹאמֵרוּ: 6ד.

Blessed be the glory of God from its place.	בָּרוּךְ כְּבוֹד־יְיָ מִמְּקוֹמוֹ. 7.

From Your place, reveal Yourself,	מִמְּקוֹמְךָ מַלְכֵּנוּ תוֹפִיעַ וְתִמְלוֹךְ עָלֵינוּ 7א.
O Sovereign, and rule over us, for we wait for You.	כִּי מְחַכִּים אֲנַחְנוּ לָךְ: 7ב.
When will You reign in Zion? Soon and	מָתַי תִּמְלוֹךְ בְּצִיּוֹן. בְּקָרוֹב בְּיָמֵינוּ 7ג.
in our days; forever may You dwell there.	לְעוֹלָם וָעֶד תִּשְׁכּוֹן: 7ד.
May You be exalted and sanctified in Jerusalem,	תִּתְגַּדַּל וְתִתְקַדַּשׁ בְּתוֹךְ יְרוּשָׁלַיִם עִירְךָ 7ה.
Your city, from generation to generation, to eternity.	לְדוֹר וָדוֹר וּלְנֵצַח נְצָחִים: 7ו.
May our eyes see Your reign established	וְעֵינֵינוּ תִרְאֶינָה מַלְכוּתֶךָ 7ז.
as was written in the songs of Your splendor,	כַּדָּבָר הָאָמוּר בְּשִׁירֵי עֻזֶּךָ 7ח.
written by the hand of David, Your righteous annointed:	עַל־יְדֵי דָוִד מְשִׁיחַ צִדְקֶךָ: 7ט.

The Eternal One shall reign forever,	יִמְלֹךְ יְיָ לְעוֹלָם, 8.
Your God, O Zion,	אֱלֹהַיִךְ צִיּוֹן, 9.
from generation to generation. Halleluyah!	לְדֹר וָדֹר. הַלְלוּיָהּ! 10.
To all generations we will tell of Your greatness	לְדוֹר וָדוֹר נַגִּיד גָּדְלֶךָ 11.
and to all eternity we will sanctify Your sacredness.	וּלְנֵצַח נְצָחִים קְדֻשָּׁתְךָ נַקְדִּישׁ. 12.
Your praise, O God, will never depart	וְשִׁבְחֲךָ, אֱלֹהֵינוּ, מִפִּינוּ לֹא יָמוּשׁ 13.
from our lips.	לְעוֹלָם וָעֶד. 14.
Blessed are You Adonai, the Sacred God.	בָּרוּךְ אַתָּה יְיָ, הָאֵל הַקָּדוֹשׁ. 15.

[ ] = omitted in some Liberal versions

TEXT EXploration

In the evening, a different קְדֻשָּׁה *is recited in every congregation.*
Practice reading this evening version.

You are sanctified and Your Name is sacred

and the devoted ones praise You every day.

Blessed are You, Eternal One, the sacred God.

1. אַתָּה קָדוֹשׁ וְשִׁמְךָ קָדוֹשׁ
2. וּקְדוֹשִׁים בְּכָל־יוֹם יְהַלְלוּךָ סֶּלָה.
3. בָּרוּךְ אַתָּה יְיָ, הָאֵל הַקָּדוֹשׁ.

Fill in the missing words from the evening version of the קְדֻשָּׁה.
Use the words found in the word family tree below.

בְּכָל־יוֹם _____ _____ וְשִׁמְךָ _____ אַתָּה

_____ יְהַלְלוּךָ סֶּלָה. בָּרוּךְ אַתָּה יְיָ, הָאֵל

Fill in the missing words from the morning version of the קְדֻשָּׁה.
You can find it on page 30 or 31. Use the words from the word family tree below.
Then fill in the three root letters in the tree's roots.

1. _____ אֶת־שִׁמְךָ בָּעוֹלָם,
2. כְּשֵׁם _____ אוֹתוֹ בִּשְׁמֵי מָרוֹם
3. כַּכָּתוּב עַל־יַד נְבִיאֶךָ:
4. וְקָרָא זֶה אֶל־זֶה וְאָמַר:
5. _____ , _____ , _____ יְיָ צְבָאוֹת,
6. מְלֹא כָל־הָאָרֶץ כְּבוֹדוֹ.
11. לְדוֹר וָדוֹר נַגִּיד גָּדְלֶךָ
12. וּלְנֵצַח נְצָחִים _____ _____.
13. וְשִׁבְחֲךָ, אֱלֹהֵינוּ, מִפִּינוּ לֹא יָמוּשׁ
14. לְעוֹלָם וָעֶד.
15. בָּרוּךְ אַתָּה יְיָ, הָאֵל _____.

שֶׁמַּקְדִּישִׁים
וּקְדוֹשִׁים
קְדֻשָּׁתְךָ
נְקַדֵּשׁ
קָדוֹשׁ
נַקְדִּישׁ
הַקָּדוֹשׁ

___ ___ ___

Yidbit

Not all Jews believe in angels, but they have been a part of our tradition since biblical times. Angels visit Abraham and Sarah to tell them they will have a child. Jacob dreams of angels going up and down a ladder, and later wrestles with one. Here are some interesting Jewish ideas about angels.

1. Angels are special creatures created by God. They are not the souls of people who have died.
2. Angels have no free will. They cannot choose for themselves.
3. There are many different kinds of angels.
   מַלְאָכִים (Messengers): They carry God's messages to people, and sometimes take human form.
   שְׂרָפִים (Seraphim): Creatures with three pairs of wings, one to help them fly, one to cover their eyes in God's presence, and one to cover their feet. They constantly sing God's praises.
   כְּרוּבִים (Cherubim): Creatures with four wings and four faces, (human, lion, ox, and eagle). They guard sacred spaces.

Prayerobics

קָדוֹשׁ, קָדוֹשׁ, קָדוֹשׁ יְיָ צְבָאוֹת, מְלֹא כָל־הָאָרֶץ כְּבוֹדוֹ.

When we recite the קְדֻשָּׁה in the morning, we are as close to God's presence as we can get. In some congregations it is customary to rise up on your toes each time you say the word קָדוֹשׁ in order to get as close to God as possible.

קָדוֹשׁ, קָדוֹשׁ, קָדוֹשׁ

Stand with your feet together.
Rise up and down on the balls of the feet.
Repeat a total of three times.

Among Ashkenazic Jews, it is also customary to look down at this moment. This helps them to go inward, and create a personal encounter with God. A different custom exists among the Sephardic Jews. When they say this line, they look up. The Sephardim teach that at this moment your face is cradled in God's hands.

Practice reciting this line from the קְדֻשָּׁה ***with these special movements.***

When we recite the קְדֻשָּׁה, we recognize that God's glory fills the world.

אוֹצַר מִלִּים
A TREASURY OF WORDS

Bon Appetit! = בְּתֵאָבוֹן!

There are times when we can see God's presence in the beauty of the world. One crisp Sunday morning, the youth group went on a field trip to look at the autumn leaves. Everyone brought a bag lunch, which they stored in a box on the bus.

After hiking through the woods and gathering leaves, everyone had quite an appetite, but when the leader pulled out the box of lunches, some of the items had fallen into the box, and Yossi's bag was completely empty. Help the youth group leader sort out the lunches by filling in the proper form of שְׁלִי, שְׁלוֹ, or שְׁלָהּ to make each sentence correct.

Personal Prayer Parchment

We all have special things, times, people and places that we set apart and infuse with meaning. There are many special Jewish times, places, and things as well. Study the Hebrew words in the Word Box and write them in the correct categories.

Jewish Things: _____

_____

Jewish Places: _____

_____

Jewish Times: _____

_____

WORD BOX

שַׁבָּת	כִּפָּה
מְזוּזָה	פֶּסַח
תְּפִלִּין	צִיצִית
טַלִּית	תּוֹרָה
סֻכּוֹת	
יְרוּשָׁלַיִם	
בֵּית-כְּנֶסֶת	
רֹאשׁ הַשָּׁנָה	
יוֹם כִּפּוּר	
אֶרֶץ יִשְׂרָאֵל	

קְדֻשָּׁה is the kind of feeling we can experience at certain times, in special places, or with people who are important to us. Close your eyes and think about a special person, place, or item. Then keep these feelings in your heart— first as you recite the silent קְדֻשָּׁה quietly to yourself, and then as you recite the public קְדֻשָּׁה aloud with your class.

Silent קְדֻשָּׁה

אַתָּה קָדוֹשׁ וְשִׁמְךָ קָדוֹשׁ וּקְדוֹשִׁים בְּכָל-יוֹם יְהַלְלוּךָ סֶּלָה.

בָּרוּךְ אַתָּה יְיָ, הָאֵל הַקָּדוֹשׁ.

Public קְדֻשָּׁה

נְקַדֵּשׁ אֶת-שִׁמְךָ בָּעוֹלָם, כְּשֵׁם שֶׁמַּקְדִּישִׁים אוֹתוֹ בִּשְׁמֵי מָרוֹם,

כַּכָּתוּב עַל-יַד נְבִיאֶךָ: וְקָרָא זֶה אֶל-זֶה וְאָמַר:

קָדוֹשׁ, קָדוֹשׁ, קָדוֹשׁ יְיָ צְבָאוֹת, מְלֹא כָל-הָאָרֶץ כְּבוֹדוֹ.

For the Jewish People, קְדֻשָּׁה is often expressed through the way we sanctify time. With this in mind, how can we bring קְדֻשָּׁה into one unique day?

"A Day Like No Other"

KEY WORD:
שַׁבָּת

דַּף קְרִיאָה
READING PAGE

Practice reading these phrases.

1. לַעֲשׂוֹת אֶת־הַשַּׁבָּת

2. וַיִּשְׁבֹּת בַּיּוֹם הַשְּׁבִיעִי

3. וַיְכַל אֱלֹהִים בַּיּוֹם הַשְּׁבִיעִי

4. וְשָׁמְרוּ בְנֵי־יִשְׂרָאֵל אֶת־הַשַּׁבָּת

5. בְּאַהֲבָה וּבְרָצוֹן שַׁבַּת קָדְשֶׁךָ

6. בָּרוּךְ אַתָּה יְיָ, מְקַדֵּשׁ הַשַּׁבָּת

7. יִשְׂמְחוּ בְמַלְכוּתְךָ שׁוֹמְרֵי שַׁבָּת

8. וַיְבָרֶךְ אֱלֹהִים אֶת־יוֹם הַשְּׁבִיעִי

9. וּבַיּוֹם הַשְּׁבִיעִי שָׁבַת וַיִּנָּפַשׁ

All of the phrases above contain a reference to שַׁבָּת. Sometimes, שַׁבָּת is called by another name. Circle all the words that come from the same root as the Key Word שַׁבָּת. Then find the phrase that means the same thing as the Key Word שַׁבָּת, and write that phrase in the calendar on the right.

	יוֹם רִאשׁוֹן
	יוֹם שֵׁנִי
	יוֹם שְׁלִישִׁי
	יוֹם רְבִיעִי
	יוֹם חֲמִישִׁי
	יוֹם שִׁשִּׁי
(יוֹם הַ_____)	שַׁבָּת

The Twelve Gates

KEY WORD:
שַׁבָּת

The blessing for Shabbat is introduced with a short passage. One or more of these introductions may be used at different times of day in different communities. Practice reading and singing these passages with your class, and answer the questions.

And the heavens and the earth were completed,	1. וַיְכֻלּוּ הַשָּׁמַיִם וְהָאָרֶץ
and all their hosts.	2. וְכָל-צְבָאָם.
And God finished on the seventh day	3. וַיְכַל אֱלֹהִים בַּיּוֹם הַשְּׁבִיעִי
all the work that God had done,	4. מְלַאכְתּוֹ אֲשֶׁר עָשָׂה,
and God rested on the seventh day	5. וַיִּשְׁבֹּת בַּיּוֹם הַשְּׁבִיעִי
from all the work that God had made.	6. מִכָּל-מְלַאכְתּוֹ אֲשֶׁר עָשָׂה.
And God blessed the seventh day	7. וַיְבָרֶךְ אֱלֹהִים אֶת-יוֹם הַשְּׁבִיעִי
and set it apart,	8. וַיְקַדֵּשׁ אֹתוֹ,
for on it God rested from all the labor	9. כִּי בוֹ שָׁבַת מִכָּל-מְלַאכְתּוֹ
that God created to make.	10. אֲשֶׁר-בָּרָא אֱלֹהִים לַעֲשׂוֹת.

1. This passage comes from the end of the first story in the Bible.

   What story does this passage tell? _____

2. Write the first word from the first line: _____

   It is the plural for "completed" or "finished." The Talmud explains that if you recite this

   paragraph on Friday evening, you become God's partner in _____ .

The Children of Israel shall keep Shabbat	1. וְשָׁמְרוּ בְנֵי-יִשְׂרָאֵל אֶת-הַשַּׁבָּת
observing Shabbat	2. לַעֲשׂוֹת אֶת-הַשַּׁבָּת
throughout their generations as an eternal covenant.	3. לְדֹרֹתָם בְּרִית עוֹלָם.
Between Me and the Children of Israel	4. בֵּינִי וּבֵין בְּנֵי יִשְׂרָאֵל
it shall be a sign forever,	5. אוֹת הִיא לְעוֹלָם,
for in six days the Eternal made	6. כִּי שֵׁשֶׁת יָמִים עָשָׂה יְיָ
the heavens and the earth,	7. אֶת-הַשָּׁמַיִם וְאֶת-הָאָרֶץ,
and on the seventh day God rested and refreshed.	8. וּבַיּוֹם הַשְּׁבִיעִי שָׁבַת וַיִּנָּפַשׁ.

3. The Hebrew word אוֹת means "a sign" or "a symbol."

   What does the passage say שַׁבָּת symbolizes? _____

Rejoice in God's reign, those who keep Shabbat	1. יִשְׂמְחוּ בְמַלְכוּתְךָ שׁוֹמְרֵי שַׁבָּת
and call it a delight.	2. וְקוֹרְאֵי עֹנֶג.
May the people who sanctify the seventh day	3. עַם מְקַדְּשֵׁי שְׁבִיעִי
all be satisfied and delighted with Your goodness.	4. כֻּלָּם יִשְׂבְּעוּ וְיִתְעַנְּגוּ מִטּוּבֶךָ.
For You favored and sanctified the seventh day	5. וְהַשְּׁבִיעִי רָצִיתָ בּוֹ וְקִדַּשְׁתּוֹ
calling it the most precious of days	6. חֶמְדַּת יָמִים אוֹתוֹ קָרָאתָ
in remembrance of creation.	7. זֵכֶר לְמַעֲשֵׂה בְרֵאשִׁית.

4. Count the Hebrew words in the above passage. _____
   This number should remind us of the number of hours
   of perfect rest and freedom Shabbat gives us.

Now, practice reading the קְדֻשַׁת הַיּוֹם *with your class.*

Our God and God of our fathers *and mothers,*	1. אֱלֹהֵינוּ וֵאלֹהֵי אֲבוֹתֵינוּ וְאִמּוֹתֵינוּ,
accept our rest.	2. רְצֵה בִמְנוּחָתֵנוּ.
Sanctify us with Your commandments,	3. קַדְּשֵׁנוּ בְּמִצְוֹתֶיךָ
and grant our portion in Your Torah,	4. וְתֵן חֶלְקֵנוּ בְּתוֹרָתֶךָ,
satisfy us with Your goodness	5. שַׂבְּעֵנוּ מִטּוּבֶךָ
and let us rejoice in Your rescue.	6. וְשַׂמְּחֵנוּ בִּישׁוּעָתֶךָ.
Purify our hearts to serve You in truth.	7. וְטַהֵר לִבֵּנוּ לְעָבְדְּךָ בֶּאֱמֶת.
Eternal our God, impart to us as our heritage	8. וְהַנְחִילֵנוּ יְיָ אֱלֹהֵינוּ
Your sacred Shabbat with love and with favor	9. בְּאַהֲבָה וּבְרָצוֹן שַׁבַּת קָדְשֶׁךָ
that all Israel, hallowing Your Name, will rest.	10. וְיָנוּחוּ בָהּ יִשְׂרָאֵל מְקַדְּשֵׁי שְׁמֶךָ.
Blessed are You, Adonai, Who sets Shabbat apart.	11. בָּרוּךְ אַתָּה יְיָ, מְקַדֵּשׁ הַשַּׁבָּת.

= added in some Liberal versions

Crack the Code

KEY WORD: שַׁבָּת

Each letter of the missing words has been coded with a number. Fill in the blanks.
Some letters have been done for you.

After creating the world, God rested on the seventh __ __ __ .

13 4 17

We rest on שַׁבָּת because God rested after creating the **W** **O** __ __ __ .

21 9 1 14 13

Shabbat__ __ __ __ __ __ at sunset on Friday, and ends on Saturday __ __ __ __ __ .

6 2 12 10 11 20   11 10 12 8 18

Because only free people can choose when to rest,

שַׁבָּת reminds us of the Exodus from __ __ __ __ __ .

2 12 17 7 18

__ __ __ __ __ __ __ שַׁבָּת is one of the Ten Commandments.

5 2 2 7 10 11 12

שַׁבָּת reminds us that __ __ __ __ is sacred.

18 10 3 2

How important is שַׁבָּת? Use the answers above to decode the message below.

__ **O** __ __   __ __ __ __ __ __ __ __ __ __ __   __ __ __   __ __ __ __

3 9 1 2   18 8 4 11 10 20 1 4 2 14   8 4 20   5 2 7 18

__ __ __ __ __ __ __ , __ __ __ __ __ __ __   __ __ __   __ __ __ __

20 8 4 6 6 4 18   20 8 4 6 6 4 18   8 4 20   5 2 7 18

__ __ __ __ __ __ . (Ahad Ha'Am, 19th Century Jewish Philosopher)

10 20 1 4 2 14

Match each activity to a word inside the Hebrew letters.
Add other activities that you feel are appropriate for שַׁבָּת.

• be with family • sing • eat challah • nap • eat festive meals • attend a Bar or Bat Mitzvah service •

pray • play games

ENJOYABLE — MOVING — FANCY — FUN

RELAXING — PLEASANT — DIFFERENT

SPECIAL — RESTFUL — ACTIVE — THINKING

read • study Torah

• stroll • eat dessert • wear best clothes • visit friends • say blessing over wine • light candles • talk •

הוֹלֵךְ / הוֹלֶכֶת   מְסִיבָה   כַּדּוּרֶגֶל

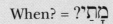
When? = מָתַי

אוֹצַר מִלִּים

A TREASURY OF WORDS

The students in Mrs. Shapiro's class all have busy schedules.
Study the two schedules below and answer the questions. Then create your own weekly schedule.

הַיּוֹמָן שֶׁל יִצְחָק	הַיּוֹמָן שֶׁל אִילָנָה
יוֹם רִאשׁוֹן	**יוֹם רִאשׁוֹן**
2:00 - הַמְּסִיבָּה שֶׁל מִיכָאֵל	2:00 - הַמְּסִיבָּה שֶׁל מִיכָאֵל
יוֹם שֵׁנִי	**יוֹם שֵׁנִי**
5:30 - גִּיטָרָה	5:30 - דְּרָמָה
יוֹם שְׁלִישִׁי	**יוֹם שְׁלִישִׁי**
4:30 - בֵּית-סֵפֶר עִבְרִי	4:30 - בֵּית-סֵפֶר עִבְרִי
יוֹם רְבִיעִי	**יוֹם רְבִיעִי**
4:00 - כַּדּוּרֶגֶל	5:30 - טֶנִיס
יוֹם חֲמִישִׁי	**יוֹם חֲמִישִׁי**
4:30 - בֵּית-סֵפֶר עִבְרִי	4:30 - בֵּית-סֵפֶר עִבְרִי
יוֹם שִׁשִּׁי	**יוֹם שִׁשִּׁי**
5:00 - עֶרֶב שַׁבָּת	5:00 - שַׁבָּת בַּבַּיִת שֶׁל סַבָּא וְסַבְתָּא
8:00 - בֵּית-כְּנֶסֶת	8:00 - בֵּית-כְּנֶסֶת
שַׁבָּת	**שַׁבָּת**
10:30 - בֵּית-כְּנֶסֶת	10:30 - בֵּית-כְּנֶסֶת

1. מָתַי הַמְּסִיבָה שֶׁל מִיכָאֵל? בְּ _____

2. מִי לוֹמֵד גִּיטָרָה? _____

3. מָתַי אִילָנָה לוֹמֶדֶת דְּרָמָה? בְּ _____

4. מָתַי הַתַּלְמִידִים בַּכִּתָּה לְעִבְרִית? בְּ _____ וְ _____

5. מָתַי הַתַּלְמִידִים בְּבֵית הַכְּנֶסֶת? בְּ _____ וְ _____

6. מִי הוֹלֵךְ לְבֵית-הַכְּנֶסֶת? _____ הוֹלֵךְ וְ _____ הוֹלֶכֶת

הַיּוֹמָן שֶׁלִּי

Write out your own weekly schedule. Complete as much of it in Hebrew as you can.

	יוֹם רִאשׁוֹן
	יוֹם שֵׁנִי
	יוֹם שְׁלִישִׁי
	יוֹם רְבִיעִי
	יוֹם חֲמִישִׁי
	יוֹם שִׁשִּׁי
	שַׁבָּת

Personal Prayer Parchment

Now that you've learned about שַׁבָּת, take a minute to record your thoughts about the קְדֻשַׁת הַיּוֹם blessing.

1. Think about a special שַׁבָּת you have experienced. What made it special?

_____

2. What could **you** do to make any שַׁבָּת special?

_____

_____

_____

Keep these thoughts in your heart as you recite the קְדֻשַׁת הַיּוֹם blessing quietly to yourself.

אֱלֹהֵינוּ וֵאלֹהֵי אֲבוֹתֵינוּ וְאִמּוֹתֵינוּ, רְצֵה בִמְנוּחָתֵנוּ.

קַדְּשֵׁנוּ בְּמִצְוֹתֶיךָ וְתֵן חֶלְקֵנוּ בְּתוֹרָתֶךָ, שַׂבְּעֵנוּ מִטּוּבֶךָ

וְשַׂמְּחֵנוּ בִּישׁוּעָתֶךָ. וְטַהֵר לִבֵּנוּ לְעָבְדְּךָ בֶּאֱמֶת. וְהַנְחִילֵנוּ

יְיָ אֱלֹהֵינוּ בְּאַהֲבָה וּבְרָצוֹן שַׁבַּת קָדְשֶׁךָ וְיָנוּחוּ בָהּ יִשְׂרָאֵל

מְקַדְּשֵׁי שְׁמֶךָ. בָּרוּךְ אַתָּה יְיָ, מְקַדֵּשׁ הַשַּׁבָּת.

= added in some Liberal versions

On Shabbat, we say the קְדֻשַׁת הַיּוֹם blessing, which asks God to help us make שַׁבָּת unique. This blessing replaces a group of Weekday Petitions, which ask God to grant our ordinary requests. These Weekday Petitions are discussed in Chapter 5.

TEXT EXploration

KEY WORD: תְּפִלָּה

The first three blessings of the עֲמִידָה are always the same, but the middle section changes. During weekday services, the central section contains 12 or 13 blessings called Petitions.

In Hebrew, the Weekday Petitions are called בַּקָשׁוֹת. Which one of the "polite words" above is from the same word family as the word בַּקָשׁוֹת? _____

What three root letters do these two words share? _____ _____ _____

The בַּקָשׁוֹת ask God to provide for three types of needs:

1. **Personal Physical Needs:** We ask God to provide the things we need to live, such as health and the ability to make a living.
2. **Personal Spiritual Needs:** The blessings in this category ask God for wisdom, forgiveness, and the ability to change the course of our lives.
3. **National Needs:** Our needs extend beyond ourselves. The Jewish people need justice, freedom, a homeland of our own, and a God who will listen to us.

Look at pages 44 or 45, and classify each Petition by category. Write the word חַי next to blessings for physical needs, draw a תּוֹרָה by those for spiritual needs, and a מָגֵן דָּוִד next to blessings for national needs.

The Twelve Gates

Read the ending phrases of the בַּקָשׁוֹת**.**

Traditional Version

Blessed are You Adonai,
    gracious Giver of knowledge. _____

בָּרוּךְ אַתָּה יְיָ, 1.
חוֹנֵן הַדָּעַת.

Blessed are You Adonai,
    who desires repentance. _____

בָּרוּךְ אַתָּה יְיָ, 2.
הָרוֹצֶה בִּתְשׁוּבָה.

Blessed are You Adonai,
    gracious and abundant in forgiveness. _____

בָּרוּךְ אַתָּה יְיָ, 3.
חַנּוּן הַמַרְבֶּה לִסְלוֹחַ.

Blessed are You Adonai,
    who rescues Israel. _____

בָּרוּךְ אַתָּה יְיָ, 4.
גּוֹאֵל יִשְׂרָאֵל.

Blessed are You Adonai,
    who heals the sick of Your people Israel. _____

בָּרוּךְ אַתָּה יְיָ, 5.
רוֹפֵא חוֹלֵי עַמּוֹ יִשְׂרָאֵל.

Blessed are You Adonai,
    who blesses the years. _____

בָּרוּךְ אַתָּה יְיָ, 6.
מְבָרֵךְ הַשָּׁנִים.

Blessed are You Adonai,
    who gathers Your scattered people Israel. _____

בָּרוּךְ אַתָּה יְיָ, 7.
מְקַבֵּץ נִדְחֵי עַמּוֹ יִשְׂרָאֵל.

Blessed are You Adonai,
    the Sovereign who loves justice. _____

בָּרוּךְ אַתָּה יְיָ, 8.
מֶלֶךְ אוֹהֵב צְדָקָה וּמִשְׁפָּט.

Blessed are You Adonai,
    who defeats the enemy and the arrogant. _____

בָּרוּךְ אַתָּה יְיָ, 9.
שֹׁבֵר אוֹיְבִים וּמַכְנִיעַ זֵדִים.

Blessed are You Adonai
    the staff and support of the righteous. _____

בָּרוּךְ אַתָּה יְיָ, 10.
מִשְׁעָן וּמִבְטָח לַצַּדִּיקִים.

Blessed are You Adonai,
    Builder of Jerusalem. _____

בָּרוּךְ אַתָּה יְיָ, 11.
בּוֹנֵה יְרוּשָׁלָיִם.

Blessed are You Adonai,
    Whose rescue will shine forth. _____

בָּרוּךְ אַתָּה יְיָ, 12.
מַצְמִיחַ קֶרֶן יְשׁוּעָה.

Blessed are You Adonai,
    who listens to prayer. _____

בָּרוּךְ אַתָּה יְיָ, 13.
שׁוֹמֵעַ תְּפִלָּה.

	Hebrew	
Blessed are You Adonai, gracious Giver of knowledge. _____	בָּרוּךְ אַתָּה יְיָ, חוֹנֵן הַדָּעַת.	1.
Blessed are You Adonai, who desires repentance. _____	בָּרוּךְ אַתָּה יְיָ, הָרוֹצֶה בִּתְשׁוּבָה.	2.
Blessed are You Adonai, gracious and abundant in forgiveness. _____	בָּרוּךְ אַתָּה יְיָ, חַנּוּן הַמַּרְבֶּה לִסְלֹחַ.	3.
Blessed are You Adonai, who rescues Israel. _____	בָּרוּךְ אַתָּה יְיָ, גּוֹאֵל יִשְׂרָאֵל.	4.
Blessed are You Adonai, who heals the sick. _____	בָּרוּךְ אַתָּה יְיָ, רוֹפֵא הַחוֹלִים.	5.
Blessed are You Adonai, who blesses the years. _____	בָּרוּךְ אַתָּה יְיָ, מְבָרֵךְ הַשָּׁנִים.	6.
Blessed are You Adonai, Redeemer of the oppressed. _____	בָּרוּךְ אַתָּה יְיָ, פּוֹדֶה עֲשׁוּקִים.	7.
Blessed are You Adonai, the Sovereign who loves justice. _____	בָּרוּךְ אַתָּה יְיָ, מֶלֶךְ אוֹהֵב צְדָקָה וּמִשְׁפָּט.	8.
Blessed are You Adonai, who will banish evil from the earth. _____	בָּרוּךְ אַתָּה יְיָ, הַמַּשְׁבִּית רֶשַׁע מִן־הָאָרֶץ.	9.
Blessed are You Adonai the staff and support of the righteous. _____	בָּרוּךְ אַתָּה יְיָ, מִשְׁעָן וּמִבְטָח לַצַּדִּיקִים.	10.
Blessed are You Adonai, Builder of Jerusalem. _____	בָּרוּךְ אַתָּה יְיָ, בּוֹנֵה יְרוּשָׁלָיִם.	11.
Blessed are You Adonai, Whose rescue will shine forth. _____	בָּרוּךְ אַתָּה יְיָ, מַצְמִיחַ קֶרֶן יְשׁוּעָה.	12.
Blessed are You Adonai, who listens to prayer. _____	בָּרוּךְ אַתָּה יְיָ, שׁוֹמֵעַ תְּפִלָּה.	13.

_____ = added in some Liberal congregations.

Yidbit

The Key Word, תְּפִלָּה, comes from a Hebrew root that means "to examine" or "to judge." The English word "prayer" comes from a Latin root that means "to beg."

What should we do during תְּפִלָּה?_____

How is the Hebrew term different from the English? _____

That Would Take a Miracle

"Settle down everyone! We have a lot to cover today." As the students found their seats, Mrs. Shapiro continued. "A couple of weeks ago Michael asked a question that I didn't answer."

"I remember," Michael said. "I asked what we were allowed to pray for."

"That's right," Mrs. Shapiro agreed. "Now, what kinds of things do you think we should ask God to do?"

"During services we ask God to cure sick people," Michael said.

"I think we can pray for people in any kind of trouble," Sarah added.

"On Yom Kippur we ask God to forgive us for the things we've done wrong," Yossi added.

"I'll bet you know those prayers by heart," Esther teased.

"Very funny Esther, but maybe you need to learn a few of them yourself." Mrs. Shapiro continued, "Are there things that we shouldn't ask of God?"

"It's not very nice to pray for revenge," Rebecca said.
"If you have a fight with someone, it's wrong to ask God to punish them. I also think it's wrong to pray for presents. God has more important things to worry about."

"On Sunday, my dad and I watched a football game," Sarah said. "The players on both teams kept praying that they'd win. I thought that was stupid because one team was going to lose anyway. I mean, does God listen more to one team than the other?"

Ilana jumped in. "Maybe they were asking God to help them do their best. There's nothing wrong with that. When Danny and Isaac were studying for that test, I think they could have asked God to help them."

"I did," Isaac confessed. "I prayed before I took it, while I was taking it, and after I'd taken it!"

"What good did that do?" Yossi asked. "Once you'd taken it, nothing was going to change your grade. That would take a miracle!"

"My cousin was driving home late one night," Danny said. "My aunt heard on the news that there had been a big accident on the road he usually takes. So she prayed that he wasn't involved in it."

"That must have been terrifying," Mrs. Shapiro said.

"It was. But my uncle said that it was useless to pray over something that had already happened."

Mrs. Shapiro nodded. "The Talmud says that praying over something that is past is making a בְּרָכָה לְבַטָּלָה, a vain or wasted prayer because changing it would require God to make a miracle just for you."

"So, Isaac," Esther asked. "Did you get your miracle?"

"I sure did," Isaac answered. "I got an 'A+'!"

Judge the Cases

Isaac's Increasing Invocations

Isaac prayed three times about his math test. Which prayers were acceptable?

1. Praying while studying before the test.
❑ Acceptable ❑ בְּרָכָה לְבַטָּלָה
Why?_____

2. Praying during the test.
❑ Acceptable ❑ בְּרָכָה לְבַטָּלָה
Why?_____

3. Praying after the test.
❑ Acceptable ❑ בְּרָכָה לְבַטָּלָה
Why?_____

Praying to Play a Part

Ilana once prayed that she would get a part in a play. What would make her prayer worthy?

_____

Danny's דּוֹדָה Despairs

What could Danny's aunt have prayed for when she heard about the accident?

_____

Rebecca Resists Revenge

Rebecca says that you should not pray for revenge. During a war, do you think one should pray for the defeat of one's enemies?
❑ Yes ❑ No

What would be a better thing to ask of God?

_____

CHAPTER 5

אוֹצֵר מִלִים
A TREASURY OF WORDS

נוֹתֵן / נוֹתֶנֶת

מִתְפַּלֵל / מִתְפַּלֶלֶת

כּוֹתֵב / כּוֹתֶבֶת

מִכְתָּב

הַכֹּתֶל הַמַעֲרָבִי

all / every = כָּל

a complete healing = רְפוּאָה שְׁלֵמָה

Give! = תֵּן

CHAPTER **5**

Language Enrichment

Check the sentence that best describes each picture.

☐ הַכֹּתֶל הַמַּעֲרָבִי בְּלוֹנְדוֹן.

☐ לוֹנְדוֹן בְּאֶרֶץ יִשְׂרָאֵל.

☐ הַכֹּתֶל הַמַּעֲרָבִי בִּירוּשָׁלַיִם.

☐ דָּנִיֵּאל כּוֹתֵב מִכְתָּב לְדוֹדָה שֶׁלּוֹ.

☐ דָּנִיֵּאל רוֹאֶה כּוֹכָבִים וְיָרֵחַ בַּלַּיְלָה.

☐ דָּנִיֵּאל שׁוֹמֵעַ רַדְיוֹ בְּעִבְרִית.

☐ יוֹסִי, תֵּן לִי אֶת הַמִּכְתָּב בְּבַקָּשָׁה!

☐ בְּתֵאָבוֹן, יוֹסִי!

☐ יוֹסִי נוֹתֵן מִכְתָּב לְמִיכָאֵל.

☐ אִילָנָה נוֹתֶנֶת חָמֵשׁ מַצּוֹת לְיוֹסִי.

☐ אִילָנָה נוֹתֶנֶת מִכְתָּב לְיוֹסִי.

☐ אִילָנָה שׁוֹמַעַת מוּסִיקָה כָּל יוֹם.

☐ שָׂרָה מִתְפַּלֶּלֶת עַל-יַד הַכֹּתֶל הַמַּעֲרָבִי.

☐ כָּל אֶחָד מִתְפַּלֵּל בְּבֵית-הַכְּנֶסֶת.

☐ שָׂרָה מִתְפַּלֶּלֶת עִם סִדּוּר.

☐ רְפוּאָה שְׁלֵמָה, יִצְחָק!

☐ חַג שָׂמֵחַ, יִצְחָק!

☐ סְלִיחָה, יִצְחָק!

Hear Our Prayers!

Earlier in the year, Danny went to visit his family in Israel. When Mrs. Shapiro heard that he was going to make the trip, she told the class about the custom of praying at the כֹּתֶל הַמַּעֲרָבִי, and placing little notes between its stones. Everyone in the class wrote notes, and Danny agreed to take them to the Wall. On his last visit to the כֹּתֶל הַמַּעֲרָבִי, he wrote his own letter, and placed it carefully between the stones. Read the letters that Danny and Sarah wrote, then help the other students finish theirs.

יְיָ אֱלֹהִים,
אֲנִי עוֹמֶדֶת בְּבֵית-חוֹלִים.
אֲנִי מִתְפַּלֶּלֶת וַאֲנִי כּוֹתֶבֶת מִכְתָּב.
יְיָ, אַתָּה רוֹפֵא חוֹלִים.
הַסַּבָּא שֶׁלִּי חוֹלֶה. אֲנִי מִתְפַּלֶּלֶת:
תֵּן רְפוּאָה שְׁלֵמָה לַסַּבָּא שֶׁלִּי.
שָׂרָה

יְיָ אֱלֹהִים,
אֲנִי עוֹמֵד עַל-יַד הַכֹּתֶל הַמַּעֲרָבִי.
אֲנִי מִתְפַּלֵּל וַאֲנִי כּוֹתֵב מִכְתָּב.
יְיָ, אַתָּה נוֹתֵן שָׁלוֹם.
אֲנִי מִתְפַּלֵּל: תֵּן שָׁלוֹם לְיִשְׂרָאֵל.
דָּנִיאֵל

יְיָ אֱלֹהִים,
אֲנִי מִתְפַּלֶּלֶת
וַאֲנִי _____ מִכְתָּב.
יְיָ, אַתָּה רוֹפֵא חוֹלִים.
אֲנִי _____:
תֵּן רְפוּאָה שְׁלֵמָה לְכָל הַחוֹלִים.
אֶסְתֵּר

יְיָ אֱלֹהִים,
אֲנִי _____
וַאֲנִי _____ מִכְתָּב.
יְיָ, אַתָּה נוֹתֵן שָׁלוֹם.
אֲנִי _____:
תֵּן שָׁלוֹם לְיִשְׂרָאֵל וּלְכָל הָעוֹלָם.
אִילָנָה

יְיָ אֱלֹהִים,
אֲנִי _____
וַאֲנִי _____ מִכְתָּב.
אֲנִי _____:
תֵּן לִי מִלְיוֹן דוֹלָרִים.
יוֹסִי

The Weekday Petitions are like writing letters to God. Look at the blessings on pages 44 and 45. What things did the kids request in their letters that we also ask for in our daily prayers?

_____

_____

Personal Prayer Parchment

Petition: *noun.* An earnest request; entreaty; especially a formal written request made to a superior.

The עֲמִידָה is like presenting a petition to God. A petition is often written, like a letter. Write a letter to God in Hebrew or English. Follow the format of the עֲמִידָה. Introduce yourself in the first paragraph. Then, write your own praise for God, similar to those found in the first three blessings of the עֲמִידָה. Next, present your requests, using the structure you discovered in the Text Exploration activity on page 43. Finally, end your letter by thanking God for all of the good things in your life.

הַמִכְתָב שֶׁלִי

Dear God,	יְיָ אֱלֹהִים,
Signed,	הַכּוֹתֵב / הַכּוֹתֶבֶת,

Just as there are Jewish ways of asking God for help, there are also Jewish ways to serve God.

CHAPTER 6

"Ask Not What God Can Do for You; Ask What You Can Do for God."

עֲבוֹדָה

KEY WORD: עֲבוֹדָה

Each of the prayer phrases that follows is missing a word related to the Key Word, עֲבוֹדָה. Fill in the blanks with words from the word family tree. Use the prayer texts on page 53.

וְהָשֵׁב אֶת-_____ לִדְבִיר בֵּיתֶךָ

וּתְהִי לְרָצוֹן תָּמִיד _____ יִשְׂרָאֵל עַמֶּךָ

פְּנֵה אֶל _____ וְחָנֵּנוּ

שְׂאוֹתְךָ לְבַדְּךָ בְּיִרְאָה _____

הָעֲבוֹדָה

נַעֲבוֹד

עֲבוֹדַת

עֲבָדֶיךָ

Serve/Work

What three letter root do all these words share?

Circle the words that share the same root letters in the Hebrew lines below. Then complete the translations.

We were _____ to the Pharaoh in Egypt.

עֲבָדִים הָיִינוּ לְפַרְעֹה בְּמִצְרָיִם.

God brought us from _____ to freedom.

הוֹצִיאָנוּ מֵעַבְדוּת לְחֵרוּת.

The Twelve Gates

Traditional Version

Adonai our God, be gracious to Your people Israel	רְצֵה יְיָ אֱלֹהֵינוּ בְּעַמְּךָ יִשְׂרָאֵל 1.
and accept their prayer; and restore the service	וּבִתְפִלָּתָם וְהָשֵׁב אֶת־הָעֲבוֹדָה 2.
of Your sanctuary; and the burnt offerings of Israel	לִדְבִיר בֵּיתֶךָ וְאִשֵּׁי יִשְׂרָאֵל 3.
and their prayers accept with love and favor.	וּתְפִלָּתָם בְּאַהֲבָה תְקַבֵּל בְּרָצוֹן. 4.
May Israel's service always be accepted.	וּתְהִי לְרָצוֹן תָּמִיד עֲבוֹדַת יִשְׂרָאֵל עַמֶּךָ. 5.
May we see Your return to Zion in mercy.	וְתֶחֱזֶינָה עֵינֵינוּ בְּשׁוּבְךָ לְצִיּוֹן בְּרַחֲמִים 6.
Blessed are You, Eternal,	בָּרוּךְ אַתָּה יְיָ, 7.
Who restores Your divine presence to Zion.	הַמַּחֲזִיר שְׁכִינָתוֹ לְצִיּוֹן. 8.

Liberal Version

Adonai our God, be gracious to Your people Israel	רְצֵה יְיָ אֱלֹהֵינוּ בְּעַמְּךָ יִשְׂרָאֵל 1.
And accept their prayers with love.	וּתְפִלָּתָם בְּאַהֲבָה תְקַבֵּל. 2.
May Israel's service always be accepted.	וּתְהִי לְרָצוֹן תָּמִיד עֲבוֹדַת יִשְׂרָאֵל עַמֶּךָ. 3.
O God Who is near to all who call,	אֵל קָרוֹב לְכָל־קֹרְאָיו, 4.
turn toward Your servants and be gracious to us.	פְּנֵה אֶל עֲבָדֶיךָ וְחָנֵּנוּ. 5.
Pour Your Spirit upon us, and	שְׁפוֹךְ רוּחֲךָ עָלֵינוּ, 6.
may we see Your return to Zion in mercy	וְתֶחֱזֶינָה עֵינֵינוּ בְּשׁוּבְךָ לְצִיּוֹן בְּרַחֲמִים 7.
Blessed are You, Eternal,	בָּרוּךְ אַתָּה יְיָ, 8.
*Whom alone we serve in awe.	*שֶׁאוֹתְךָ לְבַדְּךָ בְּיִרְאָה נַעֲבוֹד. 9.

⬜ = recited in some Traditional Congregations   = added in Liberal Congregations

*In some Liberal versions, line 8 in the Traditional version replaces this line.

Understanding the Prayer Differences

This prayer was originally part of the עֲבוֹדָה service in the ancient Temple. After the Temple was destroyed, Jews prayed for God to restore the Temple service. Early Reform Rabbis did not want the Temple service brought back since it involved sacrificing animals. They changed the words to focus on prayer and other ways of serving God.

What do you think? Check each statement with which you agree.

⬜ Sacrifices are commanded by the Torah. We should pray for their return.

⬜ Sacrifices were a way of learning to worship, but would serve no use today.

⬜ Prayer and acts of kindness are better ways of serving God.

⬜ We should remember the worship of our ancestors, and their devotion to it.

Serving God with Your Heart and Your Hands

As she entered the classroom, Mrs. Shapiro could hear the uproar. "What on earth is going on here?" she asked, placing her books on the table.

"Something terrible has happened," Michael answered. "There was a fire in my neighborhood last night, and a friend of ours lost his house!"

"I know," Mrs. Shapiro said. "It's terrible. The question is, what are we going to do about it?"

"That's the problem," Esther answered. "We thought about giving our צְדָקָה money to them, but we've only got $4.77 total. They can't do much with that."

"Maybe the other classes could donate their צְדָקָה too," Sarah suggested.

"Even with all the צְדָקָה money from the school it's not going to get them everything they need until they can find a new house," Ilana said. "It's too big a problem for us to solve. I say we should just get on with our Hebrew work."

Mrs. Shapiro frowned. "That's not always the best way of serving God."

"I know, Mrs. Shapiro!" Yossi called out. "The best way is to go to services and pray. Isn't that how we're supposed to serve God?"

"That's a very good question." Mrs. Shapiro passed out a set of worksheets. "The Rabbis called prayer, עֲבוֹדָה שֶׁהִיא בַלֵב, a service of the heart. What you need to decide is whether or not serving God with only your heart is enough."

Mrs. Shapiro's Worksheet

Help the students complete their worksheet. Study the quotations, then answer the questions.

> *"When you make many prayers to Me, I will not listen . . . Cease to do evil. Learn to do goodness. Seek justice and relieve the oppressed. Advocate for the fatherless and plead for the widow." (Isaiah 1: 15-17)*

> *"Isn't this what I require of you as a fast: to set free those who have been oppressed? Isn't it for sharing your food with the hungry, and bringing the homeless into your own house, clothing the needy when you see them, and not turning your back on your own flesh and blood?" (Isaiah 58: 6-7)*

1. The Prophet Isaiah believed that prayer and fasting, (עֲבוֹדָה שֶׁהִיא בַלֵב) were not enough. What other kinds of עֲבוֹדָה does Isaiah ask us to do to serve God?

2. What should the class do to help the family that lost its house?

מְלַמֵּד / מְלַמֶּדֶת

אוֹצָר מִלִים
A TREASURY OF WORDS

דְּבַר תּוֹרָה = sermon

Many people work hard to provide services to others.
Match each job description to the correct picture.

1. הִיא מְלַמֶּדֶת אֶת הַכִּתָּה שֶׁל אִילָנָה.

2. הִיא הָרוֹפְאָה שֶׁל מִיכָאֵל.

3. הוּא מְלַמֵּד תּוֹרָה וְתַלְמוּד. הוּא כּוֹתֵב דְּבַר תּוֹרָה.

4. הִיא נוֹתֶנֶת סְפָרִים לְכָל אֶחָד.

5. הוּא רוֹאֶה אֶת כָּל הַחוֹלִים בְּבֵית-חוֹלִים.

6. הוּא מְלַמֵּד הִסְטוֹרְיָה.

אִמָּא שֶׁל רִבְקָה רוֹפְאָה.

אַבָּא שֶׁל שָׂרָה רוֹפֵא.

אַבָּא שֶׁל רִבְקָה מוֹרֶה.

___

אִמָּא שֶׁל אֶסְתֵּר סַפְרָנִית.

הַמּוֹרָה שַׁפִּירוֹ מוֹרָה לְעִבְרִית.

אַבָּא שֶׁל יוֹסִי רַבִּי.

___

Complete the sentences.

עוֹבֵד / עוֹבֶדֶת

1. אַבָּא שֶׁל רִבְקָה _____ בְּבֵית-סֵפֶר.

2. אִמָּא שֶׁל אֶסְתֵּר _____ בְּסִפְרִיָּה.

3. אַבָּא שֶׁל יוֹסִי _____ בְּבֵית-כְּנֶסֶת.

4. הַמּוֹרָה שַׁפִּירוֹ _____ בְּבֵית-כְּנֶסֶת.

5. אַבָּא שֶׁל שָׂרָה _____ בְּבֵית-חוֹלִים.

Answer the questions.

6. אֵיפֹה הָרַבִּי עוֹבֵד? _____

7. אֵיפֹה הַמּוֹרָה לְהִסְטוֹרִיָה עוֹבֵד? _____

8. אֵיפֹה הַסַּפְרָנִית עוֹבֶדֶת? _____

9. אֵיפֹה הַמּוֹרָה לְעִבְרִית עוֹבֶדֶת? _____

10. אֵיפֹה הָרוֹפֵא עוֹבֵד? _____

Fill in the people and their jobs in the correct location. A sample has been done.

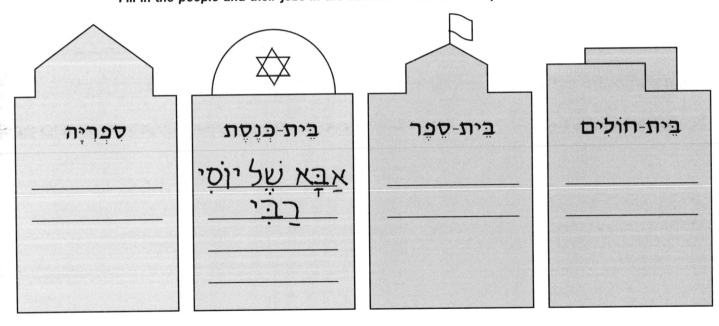

סִפְרִיָּה	בֵּית-כְּנֶסֶת	בֵּית-סֵפֶר	בֵּית-חוֹלִים
_____	אַבָּא שֶׁל יוֹסִי רַבִּי	_____	_____
_____	_____	_____	_____

Personal Prayer Parchment

KEY WORD:
עֲבוֹדָה

The עֲבוֹדָה prayer invites us to serve God. Doing things for people in need can be one of the most rewarding human experiences, and can also make us feel close to God. Think about a time when you were in trouble and someone helped you out. How did it feel? Now think of a time when you helped someone else. How did that feel? Keep these memories in your heart as you recite the עֲבוֹדָה prayer quietly to yourself.

Traditional Version

רְצֵה יְיָ אֱלֹהֵינוּ בְּעַמְּךָ יִשְׂרָאֵל וּבִתְפִלָּתָם. וְהָשֵׁב אֶת־הָעֲבוֹדָה
וְאִשֵּׁי יִשְׂרָאֵל לִדְבִיר בֵּיתֶךָ וּתְפִלָּתָם בְּאַהֲבָה תְקַבֵּל בְּרָצוֹן.
וּתְהִי לְרָצוֹן תָּמִיד עֲבוֹדַת יִשְׂרָאֵל עַמֶּךָ. וְתֶחֱזֶינָה עֵינֵינוּ
בְּשׁוּבְךָ לְצִיּוֹן בְּרַחֲמִים. בָּרוּךְ אַתָּה יְיָ, הַמַּחֲזִיר שְׁכִינָתוֹ לְצִיּוֹן.

A Liberal Version

רְצֵה יְיָ אֱלֹהֵינוּ בְּעַמְּךָ יִשְׂרָאֵל וּתְפִלָּתָם בְּאַהֲבָה תְקַבֵּל.
וּתְהִי לְרָצוֹן תָּמִיד עֲבוֹדַת יִשְׂרָאֵל עַמֶּךָ. אֵל קָרוֹב
לְכָל־קֹרְאָיו, פְּנֵה אֶל עֲבָדֶיךָ וְחָנֵּנוּ. שְׁפוֹךְ רוּחֲךָ עָלֵינוּ,
וְתֶחֱזֶינָה עֵינֵינוּ בְּשׁוּבְךָ לְצִיּוֹן בְּרַחֲמִים.
בָּרוּךְ אַתָּה יְיָ, שֶׁאוֹתְךָ לְבַדְּךָ בְּיִרְאָה נַעֲבוֹד.
* בָּרוּךְ אַתָּה יְיָ, הַמַּחֲזִיר שְׁכִינָתוֹ לְצִיּוֹן.

* In some Liberal versions, this blessing replaces the previous line.

The blessings of the עֲמִידָה can be divided into three categories: blessings of praise, blessings of petitions, and blessings of thanksgiving. The עֲבוֹדָה prayer is the first blessing of thanksgiving. In it, we thank God for giving us the ability to serve. In the next chapter, you will learn how we say thank you for all the wonderful things God does for us each and every day.

CHAPTER **6**

CHAPTER 7

"Our God Deserves Our Thanks."

הוֹדָאָה

The Twelve Gates

KEY WORD:

תוֹדָה

We give thanks to You,	1. מוֹדִים אֲנַחְנוּ לָךְ,
that You are the Eternal our God,	2. שָׁאַתָּה הוּא יְיָ אֱלֹהֵינוּ,
and the God of our fathers and mothers	3. וֵאלֹהֵי אֲבוֹתֵינוּ וְאִמּוֹתֵינוּ
forever and ever.	4. לְעוֹלָם וָעֶד.
You are the Rock of our lives, the Shield that saves us	5. צוּר חַיֵּינוּ, מָגֵן יִשְׁעֵנוּ,
in each and every generation.	6. אַתָּה הוּא לְדוֹר וָדוֹר.
We thank You and tell Your praises	7. נוֹדֶה לְּךָ וּנְסַפֵּר תְּהִלָּתֶךָ
for our lives which are in Your hands,	8. עַל חַיֵּינוּ הַמְּסוּרִים בְּיָדֶךָ,
for our souls which are in Your keeping,	9. וְעַל נִשְׁמוֹתֵינוּ הַפְּקוּדוֹת לָךְ,
for Your miracles that are with us every day,	10. וְעַל נִסֶּיךָ שֶׁבְּכָל-יוֹם עִמָּנוּ,
and for Your wonders and goodness	11. וְעַל נִפְלְאוֹתֶיךָ וְטוֹבוֹתֶיךָ
that are ever present,	12. שֶׁבְּכָל עֵת,
evening, and morning, and noon.	13. עֶרֶב וָבֹקֶר וְצָהֳרָיִם.
You are Goodness, Your compassion never ends;	14. הַטּוֹב, כִּי לֹא כָלוּ רַחֲמֶיךָ,
You are Compassion, Your kindness never fails;	15. וְהַמְרַחֵם, כִּי לֹא תַמּוּ חֲסָדֶיךָ,
You have always been our Hope.	16. מֵעוֹלָם קִוִּינוּ לָךְ.
For all these things	17. וְעַל כֻּלָּם
may Your Name be exalted and blessed	18. יִתְבָּרַךְ וְיִתְרוֹמַם שִׁמְךָ
our Sovereign, always and forever.	19. מַלְכֵּנוּ תָּמִיד לְעוֹלָם וָעֶד.
May all the living acknowledge You,	20. וְכֹל הַחַיִּים יוֹדוּךָ סֶּלָה
and praise Your Name in truth,	21. וִיהַלְלוּ אֶת שִׁמְךָ בֶּאֱמֶת,
the God Who rescues us, and helps us.	22. הָאֵל, יְשׁוּעָתֵנוּ וְעֶזְרָתֵנוּ סֶלָה.
Blessed are You, Adonai,	23. בָּרוּךְ אַתָּה יְיָ,
Whose Name is Goodness,	24. הַטּוֹב שִׁמְךָ
and to Whom our thanks are due.	25. וּלְךָ נָאֶה לְהוֹדוֹת.

= added in some Liberal versions

The הוֹדָאָה prayer reminds us about the importance of gratitude.

Turn the page to learn the Israeli way of saying "thank you."

We Give Thanks

The modern Hebrew word meaning "thank you" comes from the same root as the word מוֹדִים, the first word in the הוֹדָאָה prayer. Fill in the missing words from the הוֹדָאָה prayer. Then copy the circled letters into the lines below to discover what דָּנִיֵּאל said to thank his relatives in Israel for hosting him during his trip.

_____ ◯ ___ הוּא לְדוֹר וָדוֹר

_____ ◯ ___ לְךָ וּנְסַפֵּר תְּהִלָּתֶךָ

וְעַל נִשְׁמוֹתֵינוּ _____ ◯ ___ לָךְ

_____ ◯ ___ , כִּי לֹא תַמּוּ חֲסָדֶיךָ

_____ ◯ ___ וְיִתְרוֹמַם שִׁמְךָ

וִיהַלְלוּ אֶת שִׁמְךָ ◯ ___ ___ ___

וּלְךָ ___ ___ ◯ ___ לְהוֹדוֹת

Sometimes it is easy to say thank you. At other times it can be difficult to recognize a gift, or to see why it is important. Take a moment to explore some ideas about gifts.

For All These Things We Give You Thanks

"Now," Mrs. Shapiro said as the class finished reading the הוֹדָאָה prayer, "who can tell me what this prayer is about?"

"It's all about thanking God for all the good things we have," Michael answered.

"Okay," Mrs. Shapiro said. "So what kinds of gifts do we get from God?"

Isaac answered, "God gives us things like air, food, and water. We should be grateful for that."

"Not all food is a gift," Yossi added. "Last night my mom made liver and lima beans for dinner. There's no way I'm going to be grateful for that!"

"That's disgusting!" Esther shouted. "I wouldn't be thankful about that either."

"You raise a good point, Yossi," Mrs. Shapiro noted. "What should we do about gifts that we don't appreciate?"

"My grandparents gave me a Thesaurus for my birthday," Ilana said. "Can you imagine? It's not like they couldn't afford a good gift."

"I don't know, Ilana. I have a Thesaurus and it's really cool," Esther said. "I mean, how do you think I get all those A's in English?"

"I know what Ilana means," Rebecca said. "My grandmother sent me this awful sweater with baby ducks on it, and my mom still made me write a thank-you note for it."

"What did you say in your letter?" Mrs. Shapiro asked.

"It was hard to write because I really hated that sweater, but my mom said that I was lucky just to have grandparents at all, especially ones that really care about me. So I thanked them for thinking of me and for all their love."

"It's the thought that counts," Danny said. "Not the thing, but the person who gave it. That's a great answer, Rebecca."

"My grandpa was in the hospital right before Chanukah," Sarah said, "so he couldn't even buy me a present. But I didn't care. I got the best gift ever when he got well enough to come home."

"Maybe that's how it works with God, too," Michael said. "Maybe when we don't really like some gift, we should thank God just for thinking of us."

"If that's the case, Yossi," Esther said, "maybe you're going to have to say thank you for the liver and the lima beans!"

Describe a gift you really did not like. _____

In what way could you have been thankful for it? _____

Now, practice using Hebrew to describe God's gifts and "everyday miracles."

we = אֲנַחְנוּ	
also = גַם	
want (masc.) = רוֹצֶה	
want (fem.) = רוֹצָה	

KEY WORD: תּוֹדָה

In the הוֹדָאָה prayer, we thank God for the miracles that surround us every day. Each of the pictures below illustrates a wonder or miracle that we might take for granted. Study each picture and check the caption that best describes it.

☐ אֲנַחְנוּ תַּחַת הַיָּרֵחַ.

☐ אֲנַחְנוּ בַּשֶּׁמֶשׁ.

☐ הִיא רוֹאָה צִפּוֹר.

☐ אֲנַחְנוּ אַחִים.

☐ אֲנִי אִמָּא.

☐ אֲנַחְנוּ תַּלְמִידִים.

☐ אֲנַחְנוּ בַּכִּתָּה.

☐ אֲנַחְנוּ בְּבֵית-הַכְּנֶסֶת.

☐ הַשָּׂפָה שֶׁלִּי עִבְרִית.

☐ אֲנַחְנוּ בְּיִשְׂרָאֵל.

☐ אֲנַחְנוּ בְּנְיוּ יוֹרְק.

☐ הוּא כּוֹתֵב מִכְתָּב.

God's wonders and goodness are always present: עֶרֶב וָבֹקֶר וְצָהֳרִים

בֵּיצָה

חָלָב

אוֹצָר מִלִּים
A TREASURY OF WORDS

אֲרוּחַת עֶרֶב

אֲרוּחַת צָהֳרַיִם

אֲרוּחַת בֹּקֶר

Fill in the Hebrew names of the items on the menu.

WORD BOX			
פְּנְקֵיקְס	קָפֶה	דָּג	בֵּיצָה
סֶנְדְוִיץ'	מֵלוֹן	פִּיצָה	בֵּיגֶל
סָלַט פֵּרוֹת	סְפָּגֶטִי	סָלָט	חָלָב
תֵּה	לִימוֹנָדָה	מִילְק שֵׁיק	

שְׁתִיָּה	אֲרוּחַת צָהֳרַיִם	אֲרוּחַת בֹּקֶר
☕ _____	🐟 _____	🍳 _____
☕ _____	🥗 _____	🍔 _____
🥛 _____	🥪 _____	🥞 _____
🥤 _____	🍕 _____	🍈 _____
🧃 _____	🍝 _____	🍇 _____

אֲרוּחַת בֹּקֶר וְגַם אֲרוּחַת צָהֳרַיִם

Read the conversation and fill in Eytan's order in the waitress's notebook below.

כָּל יוֹם רִאשׁוֹן הַמִּשְׁפָּחָה שֶׁל רִבְקָה אוֹכֶלֶת אֲרוּחַת צָהֳרַיִם
בְּבֵית קָפֶה. יֵשׁ לְרִבְקָה אָח קָטָן. הַשֵּׁם שֶׁלּוֹ אֵיתָן.

אִמָּא: אֲנִי רוֹצָה סֶנְדְּוִיץ' טוּנָה בְּלִי מָיוֹנֶז בְּבַקָּשָׁה.

אֵיתָן: אֲנִי אוֹהֵב טוּנָה. אֲנִי רוֹצֶה סֶנְדְּוִיץ' עִם מָיוֹנֶז.

אִמָּא: רִבְקָה, אַתְּ רוֹצָה דָּג?

רִבְקָה: לֹא אִמָּא, אֲנִי לֹא אוֹהֶבֶת דָּג.

אֵיתָן: אֲנִי רוֹצֶה דָּג. אֲנִי אוֹהֵב דָּג עִם לִימוֹן.
אֲנִי גַּם רוֹצֶה חָלָב.

אַבָּא: אֲנִי רוֹצֶה פִּיצָה וְקָפֶה.
רִבְקָה, אַתְּ רוֹצָה פִּיצָה?

אֵיתָן: אַבָּא, הִיא לֹא אוֹהֶבֶת פִּיצָה.
אֲנִי אוֹהֵב פִּיצָה! אֲנִי רוֹצֶה פִּיצָה.

רִבְקָה: אֲנִי רוֹצָה אֲרוּחַת בֹּקֶר.
אֲנִי רוֹצָה בֵּיצָה, סָלַט פֵּרוֹת,
וְתֵה עִם חָלָב.

אֵיתָן: גַּם אֲנִי רוֹצֶה בֵּיצָה וְסָלַט פֵּרוֹת.
אֲנִי רוֹצֶה אֲרוּחַת צָהֳרַיִם
וְגַם אֲרוּחַת בֹּקֶר.

רִבְקָה: אִמָּא, אֲנִי רוֹצָה אֲרוּחַת בֹּקֶר
בְּלִי אֵיתָן.

אֵיתָן: בְּתֵאָבוֹן, רִבְקָה!

Yidbit

In Hebrew, every letter can also stand for a number. Use the chart to add up the value of מוֹדִים, the first word of the הוֹדָאָה prayer.

ו = 6	ה = 5	ד = 4	ג = 3	ב = 2	א = 1
ל = 30	כ/ך = 20	י = 10	ט = 9	ח = 8	ז = 7
צ/ץ = 90	פ/ף = 80	ע = 70	ס = 60	נ/ן = 50	מ/ם = 40
	ת = 400	ש/שׂ = 300	ר = 200	ק = 100	

ם   י   ד   ו   מ

___ + ___ + ___ + ___ + ___ = ___

According to the Talmud, one way of saying תּוֹדָה to God is reciting blessings for the things we enjoy. How does the word מוֹדִים remind us of the number of blessings we should say each day?

> *Rabbi Meir used to say, "A person must say one hundred blessings daily."* (Menachot 43b)

Prayerobics

In some congregations, people bow from the waist when saying the first word of this prayer.

It is also customary to bend the knees, bow, and rise when saying the blessing formula at the end of the הוֹדָאָה prayer.

מוֹדִים

יְיָ

אַתָּה

בָּרוּךְ

Personal Prayer Parchment

In the הוֹדָאָה prayer we thank God for all the miracles and wonders that we experience every day.

1. What is the best thing that has happened to you this week?

_____

2. What wonderful things have you seen, heard, touched, tasted, or smelled today?

_____

3. How can you say תּוֹדָה to God for all the gifts that you have received?

_____

Keep these thoughts in your mind as you recite the הוֹדָאָה prayer quietly to yourself.

מוֹדִים אֲנַחְנוּ לָךְ, שָׁאַתָּה הוּא יְיָ אֱלֹהֵינוּ, וֵאלֹהֵי אֲבוֹתֵינוּ וְאִמּוֹתֵינוּ
לְעוֹלָם וָעֶד. צוּר חַיֵּינוּ, מָגֵן יִשְׁעֵנוּ, אַתָּה הוּא
לְדוֹר וָדוֹר. נוֹדֶה לְךָ וּנְסַפֵּר תְּהִלָּתֶךָ עַל חַיֵּינוּ
הַמְּסוּרִים בְּיָדֶךָ, וְעַל נִשְׁמוֹתֵינוּ הַפְּקוּדוֹת לָךְ, וְעַל נִסֶּיךָ
שֶׁבְּכָל-יוֹם עִמָּנוּ, וְעַל נִפְלְאוֹתֶיךָ וְטוֹבוֹתֶיךָ
שֶׁבְּכָל עֵת, עֶרֶב וָבֹקֶר וְצָהֳרָיִם. הַטּוֹב, כִּי לֹא
כָלוּ רַחֲמֶיךָ, וְהַמְרַחֵם, כִּי לֹא תַמּוּ חֲסָדֶיךָ,
מֵעוֹלָם קִוִּינוּ לָךְ. וְעַל כֻּלָּם יִתְבָּרַךְ וְיִתְרוֹמַם
שִׁמְךָ מַלְכֵּנוּ תָּמִיד לְעוֹלָם וָעֶד. וְכֹל הַחַיִּים
יוֹדוּךָ סֶּלָה וִיהַלְלוּ אֶת שִׁמְךָ בֶּאֱמֶת, הָאֵל,
יְשׁוּעָתֵנוּ וְעֶזְרָתֵנוּ סֶלָה. בָּרוּךְ אַתָּה יְיָ, הַטּוֹב
שִׁמְךָ וּלְךָ נָאֶה לְהוֹדוֹת.

In the עֲמִידָה we save the most important blessing for the last. Having said thank you to God for all the gifts we receive, it's time to learn about the greatest gift of all.

= added in some
Liberal versions

CHAPTER 8
"Our God Is the God of Peace."

KEY WORD:
שָׁלוֹם

On November 4, 1995, thousands of Israelis attended a peace rally in Tel Aviv's
כִּכַּר מַלְכֵי יִשְׂרָאֵל. Before that night, there had been many demonstrations against Prime
Minister Yitzhak Rabin's peace plan.

That night, the crowd sang שִׁיר לַשָּׁלוֹם, "A Song For Peace," the anthem for supporters
of the peace process. As he was leaving the rally, Rabin was assassinated by a Jew who
opposed the peace plan. The words to this song were found in Rabin's coat pocket.

Practice reading the phrases of שִׁיר לַשָּׁלוֹם.

Let the sun rise,	תְּנוּ לַשֶּׁמֶשׁ לַעֲלוֹת,
To light up the morning,	לַבֹּקֶר לְהָאִיר,
The purest of prayers	הַזַּכָּה שֶׁבַּתְּפִלּוֹת
Will not bring us back.	אוֹתָנוּ לֹא תַּחֲזִיר.
Chorus:	פִּזְמוֹן:
So just sing a song for peace	לָכֵן, רַק שִׁירוּ שִׁיר לַשָּׁלוֹם
Don't whisper a prayer!	אַל תִּלְחֲשׁוּ תְּפִלָּה!
Better to sing a song for peace	מוּטָב תָּשִׁירוּ שִׁיר לַשָּׁלוֹם
With a great shout!	בִּצְעָקָה גְּדוֹלָה!
One whose candle has been extinguished	מִי אֲשֶׁר כָּבָה נֵרוֹ
And who is buried in the dust	וּבֶעָפָר נִטְמַן,
Will not be awakened by bitter weeping	בְּכִי מַר לֹא יְעִירוֹ,
Nor be brought back to here. (*Chorus*)	לֹא יַחֲזִירוֹ לְכָאן. (פִּזְמוֹן)
No one will bring us back	אִישׁ אוֹתָנוּ לֹא יָשִׁיב
From the deep, dark grave,	מִבּוֹר תַּחְתִּית אָפֵל,
Here the joy of victory will not help	כָּאן לֹא יוֹעִילוּ, לֹא שִׂמְחַת הַנִּצָּחוֹן
Nor will songs of praise! (*Chorus*)	וְלֹא שִׁירֵי הַלֵּל! (פִּזְמוֹן)

Circle all the Hebrew words you know. How many of them are related to light? _____

How many of them are related to prayer? _____

שָׁלוֹם רָב

שִׁיר לַשָּׁלוֹם is one of the newest songs to express Israel's hope for peace.

שָׁלוֹם רָב is one of the Jewish people's oldest prayers for peace.

שָׁלוֹם רָב is recited in the evening.

Practice reading שָׁלוֹם רָב with a partner until you can both read it fluently.

Great peace for Your people Israel	שָׁלוֹם רָב עַל-יִשְׂרָאֵל עַמְּךָ 1.
grant forever,	תָּשִׂים לְעוֹלָם, 2.
for You are the noble Sovereign of peace.	כִּי אַתָּה הוּא מֶלֶךְ אָדוֹן לְכָל הַשָּׁלוֹם. 3.
And it is good in Your sight	וְטוֹב בְּעֵינֶיךָ 4.
to bless Your people Israel	לְבָרֵךְ אֶת-עַמְּךָ יִשְׂרָאֵל 5.
and all peoples	וְאֶת-כָּל-הָעַמִּים 5א.
at every time and in every hour with Your peace.	בְּכָל-עֵת וּבְכָל-שָׁעָה בִּשְׁלוֹמֶךָ. 6.
Blessed are You, Adonai,	בָּרוּךְ אַתָּה יְיָ, 7.
Who blesses Your people Israel with peace.	הַמְבָרֵךְ אֶת-עַמּוֹ יִשְׂרָאֵל בַּשָּׁלוֹם. 8.

= added in some Liberal congregations

Many foreign dignitaries attended Yitzhak Rabin's funeral, including the leaders of Egypt, Jordan, and the United States. They had been Rabin's partners in the peace process. President Bill Clinton delivered a eulogy, and ended it by saying good-bye to his friend in Hebrew.

שָׁלוֹם, חָבֵר

KEY WORD:
שָׁלוֹם

וְטוֹב בְּעֵינֶיךָ לְבָרֵךְ אֶת-עַמְּךָ יִשְׂרָאֵל בְּכָל-עֵת וּבְכָל-שָׁעָה בִּשְׁלוֹמֶךָ.

Mrs. Shapiro called the class back together after they had practiced reading the שָׁלוֹם רָב prayer with their partners.

"I want you all to look at the line on the board. What does it mean?"

Rebecca looked back at her copy of the prayer. "It says that God always blesses Israel with peace."

"I don't get it," Yossi said. "If God really blesses Israel with peace, why is Israel always at war?"

"That's a very good question, Yossi," Mrs, Shapiro said. "What do the rest of you think about it?"

Michael spoke up. "My Mom says that she doesn't want to visit Israel because it's so dangerous there."

"I'm going to Israel with my family this summer," Sarah said. "My Dad says that Israel is safer than America."

"I agree," Danny added. "I felt really safe there. You see soldiers everywhere, but then you remember that they're Jewish soldiers. Israel has a great army, and it keeps the peace."

Mrs. Shapiro nodded. "Take a look at the last word in the line. It can be translated as 'with Your peace.' Now, what do you think that means?"

"Maybe it means that God sends us peace when we need it," Michael said.

"I think it means that God is where peace comes from," Ilana said. "Peace is always there when we need it, even in bad times, like when someone dies."

"I know what you mean," Danny said. "When I was in Israel, my aunt and uncle took me to visit the place where Yitzhak Rabin was killed. Even though a terrible thing had happened there, it was really peaceful. People from around the world have written their own messages on the walls. My aunt told me that the city council in Tel Aviv voted not to clean up the walls, but to leave the messages as a tribute to Rabin."

"Did you write a message of your own?" Esther asked.

Danny nodded. "I wanted my message to be in Hebrew, so I wrote שָׁלוֹם, חָבֵר."

Write your message to Yitzhak Rabin in Hebrew or English.

אוֹצַר מִלִים
A TREASURY OF WORDS

Many Hebrew words are related to the Key Word שָׁלוֹם.

Study the words and phrases below, then answer the questions.

How are you? (to a female) = ?מַה שְׁלוֹמֵךְ

How are you? (to a male) = ?מַה שְׁלוֹמְךָ

perfect = מֻשְׁלָם

a complete healing = רְפוּאָה שְׁלֵמָה

1. What three letters do all of these words share? _____ _____ _____

מֻשְׁלָם   שָׁלֵם   שְׁלוֹמֵךְ   שְׁלוֹמְךָ   שְׁלֵמָה   שָׁלוֹם

2. What English word is most often used to translate the Key Word שָׁלוֹם?

_____

3. What other meanings does the three letter root שׁ.ל.ם. have?

_____

4. The Key Word שָׁלוֹם is often used as a greeting and a farewell. What are
you really wishing people when you say שָׁלוֹם to them? _____

Now practice greeting people and asking how they are
using words derived from this important Key Word.

Fill in the captions with the correct form of מַה שְׁלוֹמֵךְ? *or* מַה שְׁלוֹמְךָ?.
(Hint: You can check your work by looking back to page 69.) Then number each
picture with the correct caption from the bottom of this page.

1. יוֹסִי וְהָאָב שֶׁלּוֹ בַּבַּיִת. יוֹסִי אוֹכֵל אֲרוּחַת עֶרֶב.

2. יִצְחָק לוֹמֵד גִּיטָרָה.

3. אִילָנָה הוֹלֶכֶת לָרוֹפְאָה שֶׁלָּהּ.

4. אֶסְתֵּר עַל-יַד בֵּית-הַכְּנֶסֶת. הִיא רוֹאָה אֶת שָׂרָה.

5. אֵיתָן הוֹלֵךְ לָרוֹפֵא שֶׁלּוֹ.

6. רִבְקָה שׁוֹמַעַת מוּסִיקָה. הָאֵם שֶׁלָּהּ לֹא אוֹהֶבֶת אֶת הַמּוּסִיקָה שֶׁלָּהּ.

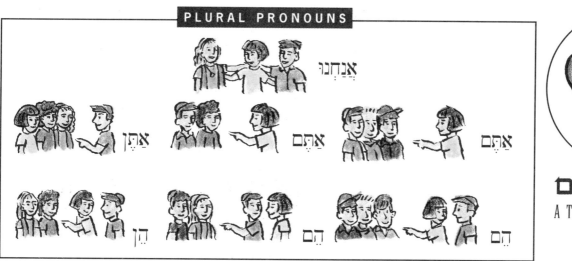

אוֹצַר מִלִים
A TREASURY OF WORDS

Help Mrs. Shapiro unmask the Purim revellers.

Write the missing pronoun in each blank to make the questions and answers correct.

Personal Prayer Parchment

Now that you've learned the שָׁלוֹם רָב prayer, take a minute to record your thoughts about our most important request.

1. What is שָׁלוֹם? _____

2. When have you felt a sense of שָׁלוֹם? _____

3. To whom would you wish שָׁלוֹם right now? _____

Keep these thoughts in your mind while you recite the שָׁלוֹם רָב prayer quietly to yourself.

Traditional Version

שָׁלוֹם רָב עַל-יִשְׂרָאֵל עַמְּךָ תָּשִׂים לְעוֹלָם, כִּי אַתָּה
הוּא מֶלֶךְ אָדוֹן לְכָל הַשָּׁלוֹם. וְטוֹב בְּעֵינֶיךָ לְבָרֵךְ
אֶת-עַמְּךָ יִשְׂרָאֵל בְּכָל-עֵת וּבְכָל-שָׁעָה בִּשְׁלוֹמֶךָ.
בָּרוּךְ אַתָּה יְיָ, הַמְּבָרֵךְ אֶת-עַמּוֹ יִשְׂרָאֵל בַּשָּׁלוֹם.

Liberal Version

שָׁלוֹם רָב עַל-יִשְׂרָאֵל עַמְּךָ תָּשִׂים לְעוֹלָם, כִּי אַתָּה
הוּא מֶלֶךְ אָדוֹן לְכָל הַשָּׁלוֹם. וְטוֹב בְּעֵינֶיךָ לְבָרֵךְ
אֶת-עַמְּךָ יִשְׂרָאֵל וְאֶת-כָּל-הָעַמִּים בְּכָל-עֵת וּבְכָל-שָׁעָה
בִּשְׁלוֹמֶךָ. בָּרוּךְ אַתָּה יְיָ, הַמְּבָרֵךְ אֶת-עַמּוֹ יִשְׂרָאֵל בַּשָּׁלוֹם.

The שָׁלוֹם רָב prayer is recited in the evening.
A different שָׁלוֹם prayer is recited in the morning.

CHAPTER 9

שִׂים שָׁלוֹם

"May God Bless You and Keep You."

KEY WORD:

בְּרָכָה

Each of the following prayer phrases is missing a word related to the Key Word בְּרָכָה. Fill in the blanks with words from the word family tree. Use the prayer texts on pages 74 and 75.

1. שִׂים שָׁלוֹם, טוֹבָה _____ _____
2. _____ _____ אָבִינוּ כֻּלָנוּ כְּאֶחָד
3. וּצְדָקָה, _____ _____, וְרַחֲמִים, וְחַיִּים, וְשָׁלוֹם.
4. וְטוֹב בְּעֵינֶיךָ _____ אֶת עַמְּךָ יִשְׂרָאֵל
5. _____ _____ אַתָּה יְיָ
6. _____ אֶת־עַמּוֹ יִשְׂרָאֵל בַּשָׁלוֹם

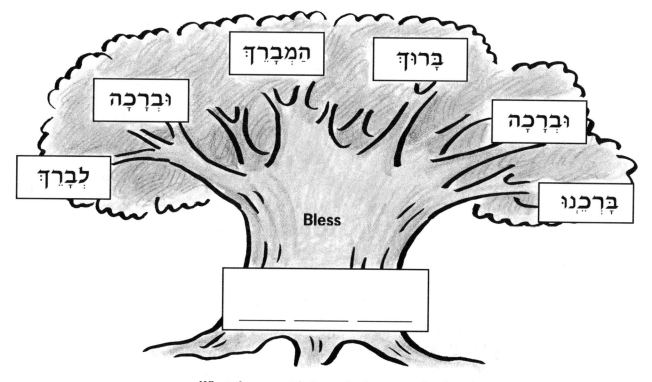

הַמְבָרֵךְ   בָּרוּךְ

וּבְרָכָה   וּבְרָכָה

לְבָרֵךְ   בָּרְכֵנוּ

Bless

_____ _____ _____

What three root letters do these words share?

Circle the words that share the same root letters in the lines below. Then complete the translations.

1. May God _____ you and keep you.   יְבָרֶכְךָ יְיָ וְיִשְׁמְרֶךָ.
2. Let us _____ Adonai Who is _____.   בָּרְכוּ אֶת־יְיָ הַמְבֹרָךְ.
3. _____ is Adonai Who is _____ forever.   בָּרוּךְ יְיָ הַמְבֹרָךְ לְעוֹלָם וָעֶד.

The Twelve Gates

Ashkenazic Orthodox Version

<table>
<tr>
<td>

Grant peace, goodness, and blessing,

grace, kindness, and compassion to us

and to all Israel, Your people.

Bless us, our Protector, one and all

In the light of Your favor.

For in that light You have given us,

Eternal our God,

the Torah of life, love of kindness,

justice, blessing, and compassion,

life, and peace.

And it is good in Your sight

to bless Your people Israel

at every time and every hour with Your peace.

Blessed are You, Adonai,

Who blesses Your people Israel with peace.

</td>
<td>

1. שִׂים שָׁלוֹם, טוֹבָה וּבְרָכָה,

2. חֵן וָחֶסֶד וְרַחֲמִים, עָלֵינוּ

3. וְעַל כָּל-יִשְׂרָאֵל עַמֶּךָ.

4. בָּרְכֵנוּ אָבִינוּ כֻּלָּנוּ כְּאֶחָד

5. בְּאוֹר פָּנֶיךָ.

6. כִּי בְאוֹר פָּנֶיךָ נָתַתָּ לָנוּ,

7. יְיָ אֱלֹהֵינוּ

8. תּוֹרַת חַיִּים, וְאַהֲבַת חֶסֶד,

9. וּצְדָקָה, וּבְרָכָה, וְרַחֲמִים,

10. וְחַיִּים, וְשָׁלוֹם.

11. וְטוֹב בְּעֵינֶיךָ

12. לְבָרֵךְ אֶת עַמְּךָ יִשְׂרָאֵל,

13. בְּכָל-עֵת וּבְכָל-שָׁעָה בִּשְׁלוֹמֶךָ.

14. בָּרוּךְ אַתָּה יְיָ,

15. הַמְבָרֵךְ אֶת-עַמּוֹ יִשְׂרָאֵל בַּשָּׁלוֹם.

</td>
</tr>
</table>

Understanding the Prayer Differences

The שִׂים שָׁלוֹם prayer asks God to grant שָׁלוֹם. Traditionally, Jews have believed that the Jewish people must help bring שָׁלוֹם to the entire world. Orthodox Jews see asking God to bless Israel with שָׁלוֹם as the first step in this process. The Conservative and Reform versions of this prayer emphasize the idea that the Jewish people desire שָׁלוֹם for all people. Which phrases did these two movements add to the prayer to make this point clear?

Conservative: _____

Reform: _____

Why is praying for world peace especially important at this point in history?

_____

A Conservative Version

Grant peace in the world,	שִׂים שָׁלוֹם בָּעוֹלָם,	1.
goodness and blessing,	טוֹבָה וּבְרָכָה	2.
grace, kindness, and compassion to us	חֵן וָחֶסֶד וְרַחֲמִים, עָלֵינוּ	3.
and to all Israel, Your people.	וְעַל כָּל־יִשְׂרָאֵל עַמֶּךָ.	4.
Bless us, our Protector, one and all	בָּרְכֵנוּ אָבִינוּ כֻּלָּנוּ כְּאֶחָד	5.
In the light of Your favor.	בְּאוֹר פָּנֶיךָ.	6.
For in that light You have given us,	כִּי בְאוֹר פָּנֶיךָ נָתַתָּ לָּנוּ,	7.
Eternal our God,	יְיָ אֱלֹהֵינוּ	8.
the Torah of life, love of kindness,	תּוֹרַת חַיִּים, וְאַהֲבַת חֶסֶד,	9.
justice, blessing, and compassion,	וּצְדָקָה, וּבְרָכָה, וְרַחֲמִים,	10.
life, and peace.	וְחַיִּים, וְשָׁלוֹם.	11.
And it is good in Your sight	וְטוֹב בְּעֵינֶיךָ	12.
to bless Your people Israel,	לְבָרֵךְ אֶת עַמְּךָ יִשְׂרָאֵל	13.
at every time and every hour with Your peace.	בְּכָל־עֵת וּבְכָל־שָׁעָה בִּשְׁלוֹמֶךָ.	14.
Blessed are You, Adonai,	בָּרוּךְ אַתָּה יְיָ,	15.
Who blesses Your people Israel with peace.	הַמְבָרֵךְ אֶת־עַמּוֹ יִשְׂרָאֵל בַּשָּׁלוֹם.	16.

A Reform Version

Grant peace, goodness, and blessing,	שִׂים שָׁלוֹם, טוֹבָה וּבְרָכָה,	1.
grace, kindness, and compassion to us	חֵן וָחֶסֶד וְרַחֲמִים, עָלֵינוּ	2.
and to all Israel, Your people.	וְעַל כָּל־יִשְׂרָאֵל עַמֶּךָ.	3.
Bless us, our Protector, one and all	בָּרְכֵנוּ אָבִינוּ כֻּלָּנוּ כְּאֶחָד	4.
In the light of Your favor.	בְּאוֹר פָּנֶיךָ.	5.
For in that light You have given us,	כִּי בְאוֹר פָּנֶיךָ נָתַתָּ לָּנוּ,	6.
Eternal our God,	יְיָ אֱלֹהֵינוּ	7.
the Torah of life, love of kindness,	תּוֹרַת חַיִּים, וְאַהֲבַת חֶסֶד,	8.
justice, blessing, and compassion,	וּצְדָקָה, וּבְרָכָה, וְרַחֲמִים,	9.
life, and peace.	וְחַיִּים, וְשָׁלוֹם.	10.
And it is good in Your sight	וְטוֹב בְּעֵינֶיךָ	11.
to bless Your people Israel,	לְבָרֵךְ אֶת עַמְּךָ יִשְׂרָאֵל,	12.
and all people,	וְאֶת־כָּל־הָעַמִּים,	13.
at every time and every hour with Your peace.	בְּכָל עֵת וּבְכָל שָׁעָה בִּשְׁלוֹמֶךָ.	14.
Blessed are You, Adonai,	בָּרוּךְ אַתָּה יְיָ,	15.
Who blesses Your people Israel with peace.	הַמְבָרֵךְ אֶת־עַמּוֹ יִשְׂרָאֵל בַּשָּׁלוֹם.	16.

Yidbit

After the עֲבוֹדָה service in the Temple, the כֹּהֲנִים or priests recited a special בְּרָכָה, called the "three-fold blessing," or הַבְּרָכָה הַמְשֻׁלֶּשֶׁת, over all the people. This ancient בְּרָכָה is found in the Torah, and was recited by Aaron and his sons. In traditional congregations, it is recited at the beginning of the שִׂים שָׁלוֹם prayer, and in some traditional congregations the כֹּהֲנִים, who are descendants of Aaron, come forward to bless the congregation.

The הַבְּרָכָה הַמְשֻׁלֶּשֶׁת is so lovely that it has become part of the בְּרָכָה some parents recite on Shabbat evening when they bless their children. Practice reading this בְּרָכָה.

May God bless you and keep you.	1. יְבָרֶכְךָ יְיָ וְיִשְׁמְרֶךָ.
May God's face shine upon you and be gracious to you	2. יָאֵר יְיָ פָּנָיו אֵלֶיךָ וִיחֻנֶּךָּ.
May God's face be lifted to you,	3. יִשָּׂא יְיָ פָּנָיו אֵלֶיךָ
and may God grant you peace.	4. וְיָשֵׂם לְךָ שָׁלוֹם.

1. What other thoughts could a parent add to this blessing?

_____

2. How might you bless your parents?

_____

TEXT EXploration

Sometimes words for the most common things are used to express poetic ideas.

Complete the translation.

פָּנִים

עֵינַיִם

your eyes = עֵינֶיךָ = שֶׁלְּךָ + הָעֵינַיִם

_____ face = פָּנֶיךָ = שֶׁלְּךָ + הַפָּנִים

In the שִׂים שָׁלוֹם prayer, two poetic ideas are expressed using words for parts of the body.
Translate and explain these phrases.

_____ בְּאוֹר פָּנֶיךָ

_____ וְטוֹב בְּעֵינֶיךָ

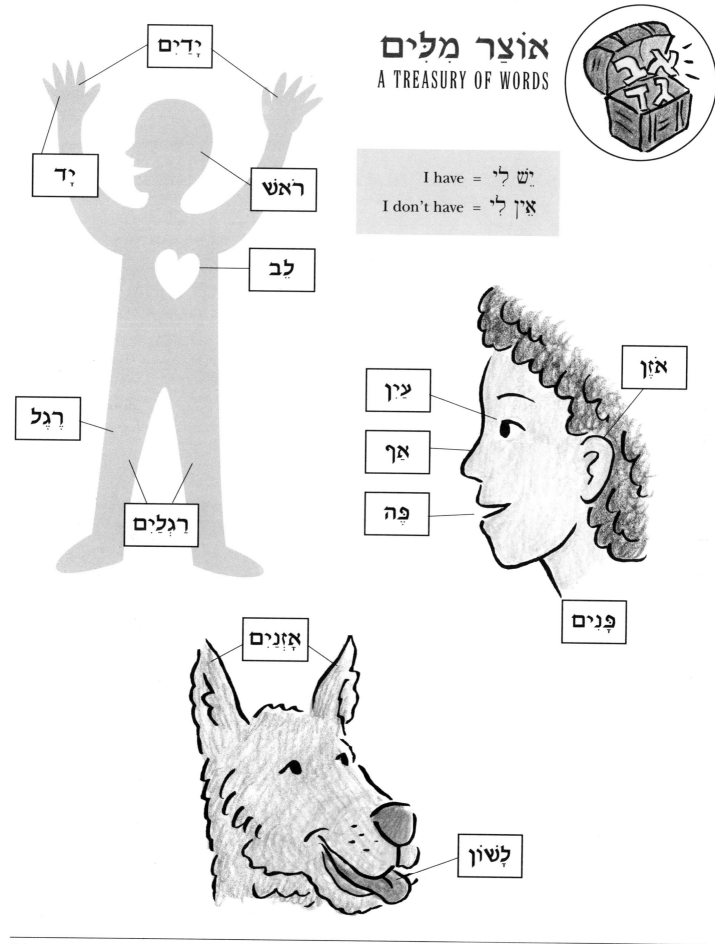

יָדַיִם

יָד

רֹאשׁ

לֵב

רֶגֶל

רַגְלַיִם

I have = יֵשׁ לִי
I don't have = אֵין לִי

אֹזֶן

עַיִן

אַף

פֶּה

פָּנִים

אָזְנַיִם

לָשׁוֹן

Under each picture, write the number of the sentence that matches it.

1. יֵשׁ לִי אַף גָּדוֹל.

2. אֵין לִי עַיִן.

3. יֵשׁ לִי פֶּה גָּדוֹל.

4. יֵשׁ לִי שְׁמוֹנֶה רַגְלַיִם.

5. יֵשׁ לִי אֹזֶן גְּדוֹלָה.

6. יֵשׁ לִי לָשׁוֹן גְּדוֹלָה.

7. יֵשׁ לִי שָׁלוֹשׁ עֵינַיִם.

8. יֵשׁ לִי יָד עַל הַלֵּב.

_____

_____

_____

_____

_____

_____

_____

_____

To Be or Not to Be

אוֹצַר מִלִים
A TREASURY OF WORDS

want (fem.) = רוֹצָה   want (masc.) = רוֹצֶה

The prefix -לְ means "to" or "for." When it is added at the beginning of a verb, the verb's spelling changes a little. Study each of the verbs that you already know, then fill in the blanks to provide translations of the new verb forms.

to _____ = לַעֲמֹד   עוֹמֵד/עוֹמֶדֶת

to _____ = לִכְתֹּב   כּוֹתֵב/כּוֹתֶבֶת

to _____ = לֶאֱכֹל   אוֹכֵל/אוֹכֶלֶת

to _____ = לִשְׁמֹעַ   שׁוֹמֵעַ/שׁוֹמַעַת

to _____ = לָלֶכֶת   הוֹלֵךְ/הוֹלֶכֶת

to _____ = לְהִתְפַּלֵל   מִתְפַּלֵל/מִתְפַּלֶלֶת

Fill in the blank with the number of the caption that best describes each picture.

1. רִבְקָה אוֹכֶלֶת אֲרוּחַת צָהֳרַיִם. אִילָנָה רוֹצָה לֶאֱכֹל.

2. שָׂרָה מִתְפַּלֶּלֶת בְּבֵית-הַכְּנֶסֶת. אָדָם לֹא רוֹצֶה לְהִתְפַּלֵּל.

3. אֶסְתֵּר שׁוֹמַעַת מוּסִיקָה. תָּמִי רוֹצָה לִשְׁמֹעַ.

4. מִיכָאֵל הוֹלֵךְ לַבַּיִת שֶׁל יִצְחָק. הַכֶּלֶב שֶׁלוֹ רוֹצֶה לָלֶכֶת.

5. דָּנִיאֵל עוֹמֵד בַּכִּתָּה. הוּא רוֹצֶה לַעֲמֹד בִּירוּשָׁלַיִם.

6. הַמּוֹרָה שַׁפִּירוֹ כּוֹתֶבֶת עַל הַלּוּחַ. יוֹסִי רוֹצֶה לִכְתֹּב.

_____

_____

_____

_____

_____

_____

Personal Prayer Parchment

The שִׂים שָׁלוֹם prayer asks God to grant
שָׁלוֹם to the Jewish people.
How would you bring שָׁלוֹם into the world?

_____

_____

Keep these thoughts in your heart while you recite the שִׂים שָׁלוֹם prayer quietly to yourself.

A Conservative Version

שִׂים שָׁלוֹם בָּעוֹלָם טוֹבָה וּבְרָכָה, חֵן וָחֶסֶד וְרַחֲמִים, עָלֵינוּ וְעַל כָּל-יִשְׂרָאֵל
עַמֶּךָ. בָּרְכֵנוּ אָבִינוּ כֻּלָּנוּ כְּאֶחָד בְּאוֹר פָּנֶיךָ. כִּי בְאוֹר פָּנֶיךָ נָתַתָּ לָנוּ, יְיָ
אֱלֹהֵינוּ תּוֹרַת חַיִּים וְאַהֲבַת חֶסֶד, וּצְדָקָה, וּבְרָכָה, וְרַחֲמִים, וְחַיִּים,
וְשָׁלוֹם. וְטוֹב בְּעֵינֶיךָ לְבָרֵךְ אֶת עַמְּךָ יִשְׂרָאֵל, בְּכָל עֵת וּבְכָל שָׁעָה
בִּשְׁלוֹמֶךָ. בָּרוּךְ אַתָּה יְיָ, הַמְבָרֵךְ אֶת-עַמּוֹ יִשְׂרָאֵל בַּשָּׁלוֹם.

A Reform Version

שִׂים שָׁלוֹם, טוֹבָה וּבְרָכָה חֵן וָחֶסֶד וְרַחֲמִים, עָלֵינוּ וְעַל כָּל-יִשְׂרָאֵל עַמֶּךָ.
בָּרְכֵנוּ אָבִינוּ כֻּלָּנוּ כְּאֶחָד בְּאוֹר פָּנֶיךָ. כִּי בְאוֹר פָּנֶיךָ נָתַתָּ לָנוּ, יְיָ
אֱלֹהֵינוּ תּוֹרַת חַיִּים, וְאַהֲבַת חֶסֶד, וּצְדָקָה, וּבְרָכָה, וְרַחֲמִים, וְחַיִּים,
וְשָׁלוֹם. וְטוֹב בְּעֵינֶיךָ לְבָרֵךְ אֶת עַמְּךָ יִשְׂרָאֵל, וְאֶת-כָּל-הָעַמִּים, בְּכָל
עֵת וּבְכָל שָׁעָה בִּשְׁלוֹמֶךָ. בָּרוּךְ אַתָּה יְיָ, הַמְבָרֵךְ אֶת-עַמּוֹ יִשְׂרָאֵל בַּשָּׁלוֹם.

ONE SHOULD NOT MAKE ONE'S PRAYER A FIXED TASK.
Rabbi Eliezer says, "When is prayer a fixed task?" . . .
Rabbah and Rabbi Yosef both say: "Whenever you are not
able to add something fresh to it." (Berachot 29b)

Originally, the עֲמִידָה ended with the prayer for שָׁלוֹם. But the Rabbis
taught that each person should add something unique to his or her prayers.
Many Rabbis wrote their own meditations which they recited at the end of the
עֲמִידָה to make it more personal. Now that you have learned all the blessings
of the עֲמִידָה, it is time to make it *your* prayer.

CHAPTER 10

"May God Guard My Tongue from Evil."

אֱלֹהַי נְצוֹר

KEY WORD:
לָשׁוֹן

The עֲמִידָה both begins and ends with lines from the Psalms which ask God to help us use our speech wisely. Read the line that follows, and draw a mouth above the Hebrew word that means "my mouth," and a heart above the Hebrew word for "my heart."

יִהְיוּ לְרָצוֹן אִמְרֵי פִי, וְהֶגְיוֹן לִבִּי לְפָנֶיךָ, יְיָ צוּרִי וְגוֹאֲלִי.

Now practice this prayer until you can read it fluently.

My God, guard my tongue from evil,	אֱלֹהַי, נְצוֹר לְשׁוֹנִי מֵרָע,	1.
and my lips from speaking deceit.	וּשְׂפָתַי מִדַּבֵּר מִרְמָה.	2.
Let me pay no heed to those who speak ill of me,	וְלִמְקַלְלַי נַפְשִׁי תִדּוֹם,	3.
that my soul may be humble to all.	וְנַפְשִׁי כֶּעָפָר לַכֹּל תִּהְיֶה.	4.
Open my heart to Your Torah,	פְּתַח לִבִּי בְּתוֹרָתֶךָ,	5.
that my soul may pursue Your Mitzvot.	וּבְמִצְוֹתֶיךָ תִּרְדּוֹף נַפְשִׁי,	6.
And those who think evil about me	וְכָל הַחוֹשְׁבִים עָלַי רָעָה	7.
speedily annul their plots,	מְהֵרָה הָפֵר עֲצָתָם	8.
and spoil their plans.	וְקַלְקֵל מַחֲשַׁבְתָּם.	9.
Do this for the sake of Your Name.	עֲשֵׂה לְמַעַן שְׁמֶךָ,	10.
Do this for the sake of Your right hand.	עֲשֵׂה לְמַעַן יְמִינֶךָ,	11.
Do this for the sake of Your Holiness.	עֲשֵׂה לְמַעַן קְדֻשָּׁתֶךָ,	12.
Do this for the sake of Your Torah.	עֲשֵׂה לְמַעַן תּוֹרָתֶךָ.	13.
For the sake of delivering Your beloved,	לְמַעַן יֵחָלְצוּן יְדִידֶיךָ,	14.
rescue Your supporter, and answer me.	הוֹשִׁיעָה יְמִינְךָ וַעֲנֵנִי.	15.
May the words of my mouth,	יִהְיוּ לְרָצוֹן אִמְרֵי פִי,	16.
and the meditations of my heart be acceptable to You,	וְהֶגְיוֹן לִבִּי לְפָנֶיךָ,	17.
Adonai my Rock and my Redeemer.	יְיָ צוּרִי וְגוֹאֲלִי.	18.
May the One Who makes peace in the heavens,	עֹשֶׂה שָׁלוֹם בִּמְרוֹמָיו,	19.
make peace for us	הוּא יַעֲשֶׂה שָׁלוֹם עָלֵינוּ	20.
and for all Israel.	וְעַל כָּל יִשְׂרָאֵל.	21.
And let us say, Amen.	וְאִמְרוּ אָמֵן.	22.

Like Feathers in the Wind

When Mrs. Shapiro came into the room, her smile was bigger than usual. "Sorry I'm late, but before we review the concluding prayer of the עֲמִידָה, does anyone know where Yossi is?"

"He's in real trouble this time," Michael said. "This morning, he was called to the principal's office, and then the secretary came in and got his bookbag."

"I think he's finally been suspended," Ilana added. "I saw him getting into his dad's car, and he looked pretty worried. Maybe they finally figured out that he's the one who is pulling the fire alarms."

"I don't think Yossi's doing that," Danny said. "He and I were both in the lunchroom the last time it happened."

Ilana tossed her hair. "Well then, maybe it was for being disrespectful to the teachers. He's always talking back, and doing things to disrupt class. Last week he put a rubber snake in the librarian's desk drawer. She nearly had a heart attack when she saw it. Maybe they finally got sick of it."

Rebecca laughed. "That's true. He's always doing something to make everyone laugh, but you don't get suspended for just goofing off."

Mrs. Shapiro frowned. "I'm a little unhappy with the tone of this discussion. This is what Jewish tradition calls לָשׁוֹן הָרַע, gossip, and it's exactly what the prayer we are studying tells us to avoid."

Ilana moaned. "But Mrs. Shapiro, everybody gossips!"

Mrs. Shapiro's voice was soft and low. "Let me ask you this, Ilana, has anyone ever told tales about you?"

Ilana squirmed in her seat. "Well, yeah . . ."

"So you know how awful it made you feel. In the Talmud, the Rabbis equate gossip with murder," Mrs. Shapiro continued. "They say that לָשׁוֹן הָרַע kills three people: the one who spreads it, the one who hears it, and especially the one it is about."

"No way!" Esther called out. "How could they possibly think that a little gossip is like murder?"

"Because your reputation is the most important thing you have; the one thing you really own. לָשׁוֹן הָרַע takes that away from you, and destroys it. And once it's gone, it can never be restored, just like a life can never be restored."

"Couldn't you just apologize to the person you've wronged?" Esther asked.

"What about all the people you told?" Sarah asked. "Won't they still think the story is true?"

"Okay," Esther added. "So you apologize to the person, and tell everyone you told that you were wrong."

"There is a Hasidic story that illustrates just how difficult that can really be," Mrs. Shapiro said.

There was once a man who spread stories about his neighbor all around the town. When he realized what a terrible thing he had done he went to his Rabbi, and asked what he could do to make up for his error. The Rabbi said, "Take a feather pillow, cut it open, and scatter the feathers all over town." The man did this, and returned to the Rabbi with an empty pillow.

"Now," said the Rabbi, "go and collect all the feathers again. When you have them all back in the pillow the damage will be undone."

"I can't do that," cried the man. "The wind has scattered the feathers all over. I'll never be able to get all of them back."

"So it is with gossip," replied the Rabbi. "Gossiping about someone is like scattering feathers in the wind. It is almost impossible to take it back."

At that moment, Yossi burst into the room. "Sorry I'm late, Mrs. Shapiro. Did you tell them the news?"

"No, Yossi. Everyone was quite concerned about you, since you left school so unexpectedly this morning. Why don't you tell them where you've been."

"I was at the hospital," Yossi announced. "My mom just had a baby. I have a new little brother!"

"Hey Ilana," Danny called out. "Do you want to borrow my pillow?"

Help Ilana undo the damage she's done to Yossi.
Write the words she needs to tell everyone.

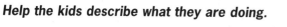

do or make (masc. sing.) =	עוֹשֶׂה
do or make (fem. sing) =	עוֹשָׂה

Help the kids describe what they are doing.

Fill in the blanks with the correct forms of the verbs found in the box.

WORD BOX

אוֹכֶלֶת	אוֹכֵל	עוֹמֶדֶת	עוֹמֵד
כּוֹתֶבֶת	כּוֹתֵב	הוֹלֶכֶת	הוֹלֵךְ
מִתְפַּלֶּלֶת	מִתְפַּלֵּל	נוֹתֶנֶת	נוֹתֵן

Fill in the blanks with the correct form, עוֹשֶׂה or עוֹשָׂה.

Yidbit

(YOUR NAME GOES HERE!)

יִהְיוּ לְרָצוֹן אִמְרֵי פִי, וְהֶגְיוֹן לִבִּי לְפָנֶיךָ, יְיָ צוּרִי וְגוֹאֲלִי.

עֹשֶׂה שָׁלוֹם בִּמְרוֹמָיו, הוּא יַעֲשֶׂה שָׁלוֹם עָלֵינוּ וְעַל כָּל יִשְׂרָאֵל. וְאִמְרוּ אָמֵן.

There is a wonderful tradition that allows us to personalize our prayers at the end of the עֲמִידָה. For every Hebrew name there is a biblical verse. This verse begins with the first letter of the name, and ends with its last letter. Reciting your verse at the end of the עֲמִידָה is like adding your personal signature to your prayer.

1. Look up your name's verse, and write it here (your teacher has a list):

_____

_____

2. Using your personal verse, design an emblem for yourself that expresses your individuality.

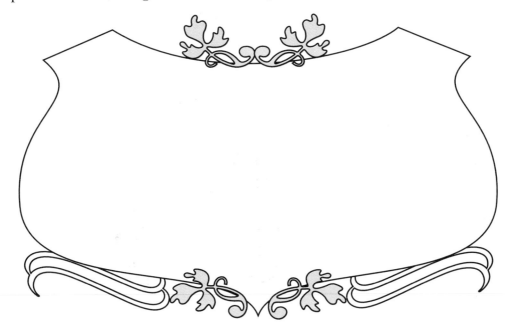

3. Practice reciting your verse before the two closing sentences of the עֲמִידָה until you can recite it fluently.

(YOUR NAME GOES HERE!)

יִהְיוּ לְרָצוֹן אִמְרֵי פִי, וְהֶגְיוֹן לִבִּי לְפָנֶיךָ, יְיָ צוּרִי וְגוֹאֲלִי.

עֹשֶׂה שָׁלוֹם בִּמְרוֹמָיו, הוּא יַעֲשֶׂה שָׁלוֹם עָלֵינוּ וְעַל כָּל יִשְׂרָאֵל. וְאִמְרוּ אָמֵן.

Prayerobics

KEY WORD:
לָשׁוֹן

When we recite the conclusion of the עֲמִידָה, we are leaving God's royal court. Just as there are precise steps for entering God's court, a formal process for leaving God's presence is used in congregations where the עֲמִידָה is recited silently. Here's how it works.

1. Bow forward. Then, beginning with the left foot, take three small steps backwards. On the last step, put your feet together, bow to the left, and say:

עֹשֶׂה שָׁלוֹם בִּמְרוֹמָיו

2. Bow to the right and say:

הוּא יַעֲשֶׂה שָׁלוֹם עָלֵינוּ

3. Bow to the center and say:

וְעַל כָּל יִשְׂרָאֵל. וְאִמְרוּ אָמֵן.

4. Rise up straight.

This special kind of bow reminds us that God is everywhere. Now that you can read this conclusion fluently, practice reading it with the special steps that accompany it until you can coordinate your words and actions.

עֹשֶׂה שָׁלוֹם בִּמְרוֹמָיו, הוּא יַעֲשֶׂה שָׁלוֹם עָלֵינוּ וְעַל כָּל יִשְׂרָאֵל. וְאִמְרוּ אָמֵן.

Personal Prayer Parchment

As you prepare to leave God's royal court, take a few moments to record your thoughts about the concluding prayer of the עֲמִידָה.

The אֱלֹהַי נְצוֹר prayer reminds us about the power of language. In it we seek God's help in making sure that we never use our power of speech for evil purposes. We also ask God to protect us from those who think and speak ill of us. Jewish tradition teaches that sticks and stones can only break our bones, but cruel words can hurt the soul.

> מָוֶת וְחַיִּים בְּיַד-לָשׁוֹן.
>
> *"Death and life are in the power of the tongue."* (Proverbs 18:21)

1. What kinds of words make the world a better place?

   Words that _____

   _____

2. What kinds of words bring harm into the world?

   Words that _____

   _____

Keep these thoughts in your heart and mind as you recite the אֱלֹהַי נְצוֹר prayer quietly to yourself.

אֱלֹהַי, נְצוֹר לְשׁוֹנִי מֵרָע, וּשְׂפָתַי מִדַּבֵּר מִרְמָה. וְלִמְקַלְלַי נַפְשִׁי
תִדֹּם, וְנַפְשִׁי כֶּעָפָר לַכֹּל תִּהְיֶה. פְּתַח לִבִּי בְּתוֹרָתֶךָ, וּבְמִצְוֹתֶיךָ
תִּרְדּוֹף נַפְשִׁי, וְכָל הַחוֹשְׁבִים עָלַי רָעָה מְהֵרָה הָפֵר עֲצָתָם וְקַלְקֵל
מַחֲשַׁבְתָּם. עֲשֵׂה לְמַעַן שְׁמֶךָ, עֲשֵׂה לְמַעַן יְמִינֶךָ, עֲשֵׂה לְמַעַן
קְדֻשָּׁתֶךָ, עֲשֵׂה לְמַעַן תּוֹרָתֶךָ. לְמַעַן יֵחָלְצוּן יְדִידֶיךָ, הוֹשִׁיעָה
יְמִינְךָ וַעֲנֵנִי. יִהְיוּ לְרָצוֹן אִמְרֵי פִי, וְהֶגְיוֹן לִבִּי לְפָנֶיךָ, יְיָ צוּרִי
וְגוֹאֲלִי. עֹשֶׂה שָׁלוֹם בִּמְרוֹמָיו, הוּא יַעֲשֶׂה שָׁלוֹם עָלֵינוּ וְעַל כָּל
יִשְׂרָאֵל. וְאִמְרוּ אָמֵן.

עֲמִידָה Wrap-Up

Now that you've learned the whole עֲמִידָה, take some time to review this important section of the service.

1. The עֲמִידָה begins and ends with a reminder that _____ is important.

2. There are three categories of prayers in the עֲמִידָה: praise, petition, and thanksgiving. Complete the chart to classify each blessing found in the עֲמִידָה.

Blessing	Pages	Belongs in the . . . category	Because
אָבוֹת	10 - 11		
גְּבוּרוֹת	22 - 23		
קְדֻשָּׁה	30 - 31		
קְדֻשַּׁת הַיּוֹם ----- or ----- בַּקָּשׁוֹת	37 - 38 44 - 45		
עֲבוֹדָה	53		
הוֹדָאָה	58		
שָׁלוֹם רָב ----- or ----- שִׂים שָׁלוֹם	67 74 - 75		

3. During the עֲמִידָה, we see ourselves as if we were appearing before God's royal court. If you could ask God for anything, what would you request?

Keep all of these thoughts in your mind while you recite the entire עֲמִידָה quietly to yourself.

Key Word WORD SEARCH

By now your Hebrew has gotten so good that you can define the Key Words from this book in Hebrew.

1. יְיָ שׁוֹמֵעַ ____ ____ ____ ____ .

2. ____ ____ ____ ____ שֶׁהִיא בַּלֵּב. (what the Rabbis called prayer)

3. בְּבַקָּשָׁה וְ____ ____ ____ ____ . (the "magic" words in Hebrew)

4. אַבְרָהָם, יִצְחָק, וְיַעֲקֹב הֵם ____ ____ ____ ____ .

5. ____ ____ ____ = יוֹם הַשְּׁבִיעִי

6. עִבְרִית הַ____ ____ ____ שֶׁל יִשְׂרָאֵל.

7. "הַמּוֹצִיא לֶחֶם" הִיא הַ____ ____ ____ ____ עַל הַלֶּחֶם.

8. יוֹנִי נְתַנְיָהוּ ____ ____ ____ ____ .

9. ____ ____ ____ ____ , חָבֵר. (President Clinton said this at Rabin's funeral)

10. ____ ____ ____ הָרָע (the Rabbis said it kills three)

11. ____ ____ ____ , קָדוֹשׁ, קָדוֹשׁ (rise up singing)

(Hint: If you need help, look at pages 5, 13, 21, 36, 45, 54, 59, 67, 73, and 83.)

Find the words you have written above and circle them in the puzzle below.

Now that you have almost completed this book, it's time to look ahead to the topic of the next book in your Hebrew program. Find and circle the Key Words in the puzzle to discover the service that you will be studying in Book 4. (Bonus question: which Key Word does *not* appear in this puzzle? _____)

ע	מ	ה	נ	ק	ר	ה	ד	נ	ה	צ	ד	ו	מ	ע	ה	מ	ד	פ	ס
ק	ם	ו	ל	שׁ	א	ר	ו	ב	ג	ח	ע	ח	ק	ב	ת	ו	ב	א	ה
ה	ו	כ	ה	ב	ת	פ	ן	ז	ל	ה	ב	שׁ	פ	ו	ו	ו	צ	ד	ת	ו
ד	שׁ	ם	ק	ר	ה	מ	ז	ל	שׁ	ץ	ו	ט	ה	מ	ד	כ	ח	פ	ן
פ	ב	ב	נ	כ	ר	ב	ל	ן	ו	ד	ד	ח	נ	צ	ה	ח	נ	ל	מ
ו	ת	ס	ה	ה	ק	פ	ע	צ	ן	ח	ה	ה	ה	פ	שׁ	ה	ו	ה	ח
מ	ה	ה	ת	שׁ	ט	ד	ם	כ	ה	ץ	ק	נ	ח	כ	ם	ה	ת	ז	ק	ע

Mrs. Shapiro's Bulletin Board

Mrs. Shapiro's class created a bulletin board to demonstrate their Hebrew skills.
The students brought in pictures, and wrote captions for each.
Find the best caption for each picture, and write its number in the space beneath the picture.

מַה מִיכָאֵל אוֹהֵב?

_____

מָה אֶסְתֵּר עוֹשָׂה?

_____

מַה דָּנִיאֵל עוֹשֶׂה?

_____

מַה הַמּוֹרָה שָׁפִירוֹ עוֹשָׂה?

_____

מָה רִבְקָה רוֹצָה?

_____

אֵיפֹה אַתֶּם?

_____

מַה יוֹסִי עוֹשֶׂה?

_____

1. הוּא רוֹאֶה אֶת הָאָח שֶׁלוֹ.
2. אֲנַחְנוּ בַּפִּיקְנִיק.
3. הוּא אוֹהֵב כַּדּוּרֶגֶל.
4. הִיא אוֹכֶלֶת אֲרוּחַת צָהֳרַיִם.
5. הִיא מְלַמֶּדֶת עִבְרִית.
6. הִיא רוֹצָה לִכְתֹּב מִכְתָּב לַדּוֹדָה שֶׁלָּה.
7. הוּא מִתְפַּלֵּל עַל-יַד הַכֹּתֶל הַמַּעֲרָבִי עִם הַדּוֹד שֶׁלוֹ.

Dictionary   מִלּוֹן

א

	Chapter	Hebrew
___	(1)	אָב
dad		אַבָּא
___	(1)	אָבוֹת
love (masc. sing.)		אוֹהֵב
love (fem. sing.)		אוֹהֶבֶת
eat (masc. sing.)		אוֹכֵל
eat (fem. sing.)		אוֹכֶלֶת
light		אוֹר
___	(9)	אֹזֶן
___	(9)	אָזְנַיִם
___	(1)	אָח
one (masc.)		אֶחָד
___	(1)	אָחוֹת
one (fem.)		אַחַת
___	(Intro.)	אִידִיש
there is not		אֵין
___	(9)	אֵין לִי
where?		אֵיפֹה
___	(1)	אִם
mom		אִמָּא
___	(7)	אֲנַחְנוּ
I		אֲנִי
___	(9)	אַף
zero		אֶפֶס
four (fem.)		אַרְבַּע
___	(7)	אֲרוּחַת בֹּקֶר
___	(7)	אֲרוּחַת עֶרֶב
___	(7)	אֲרוּחַת צָהֳרַיִם

	Chapter	Hebrew
land		אֶרֶץ
you (fem. sing.)		אַתְּ
you (masc. sing.)		אַתָּה
___	(8)	אַתֶּם
___	(8)	אַתֶּן

ב

		Hebrew
in		בְּ-
please		בְּבַקָשָׁה
___	(7)	בֵּיצָה
house		בַּיִת
___	(2)	בֵּית חוֹלִים
synagogue		בֵּית-כְּנֶסֶת
school		בֵּית-סֵפֶר
cafe		בֵּית-קָפֶה
without		בְּלִי
___	(1)	בֵּן
morning		בֹּקֶר
good morning		בֹּקֶר טוֹב
___	(9)	בְּרָכָה
___	(1)	בַּת
___	(3)	בְּתֵאָבוֹן!

ג

		Hebrew
___	(2)	גִּבּוֹר
___	(2)	גְּבוּרָה
big (masc. sing.)		גָּדוֹל
big (fem. sing.)		גְּדוֹלָה
___	(7)	גַּם

Dictionary / מִלּוֹן

Chapter	Hebrew		Chapter	Hebrew
	ד		Thursday	יוֹם חֲמִישִׁי
(6)	דְּבַר תּוֹרָה		Sunday	יוֹם רִאשׁוֹן
fish	דָּג		Wednesday	יוֹם רְבִיעִי
(1)	דּוֹד		Tuesday	יוֹם שְׁלִישִׁי
(1)	דּוֹדָה		Monday	יוֹם שֵׁנִי
	ה		Friday	יוֹם שִׁשִּׁי
he	הוּא		moon	יָרֵחַ
(4)	הוֹלֵךְ		there is	יֵשׁ
(4)	הוֹלֶכֶת		(1)	יֵשׁ לִי
she	הִיא		Israel	יִשְׂרָאֵל
(5)	הַכֹּתֶל הַמַּעֲרָבִי			**כ**
(8)	הֵם		(4)	כַּדּוּרֶגֶל
(8)	הֵן		star	כּוֹכָב
	ח		(5)	כּוֹתֵב
happy holiday	חַג שָׂמֵחַ		(5)	כּוֹתֶבֶת
(2)	חוֹלֶה		all, every	כָּל
(2)	חוֹלָה		dog	כֶּלֶב
ill people	חוֹלִים		how many?	כַּמָּה
Cantor	חַזָּן		yes	כֵּן
(7)	חָלָב		classroom	כִּתָּה
five (fem.)	חָמֵשׁ			**ל**
	ט		to, for	לְ-
good (masc. sing.)	טוֹב		no	לֹא
good (fem. sing.)	טוֹבָה		(Intro.)	לָאדִינוֹ
	י		(9)	לֵב
hand	יָד		black board	לוּחַ
hands	יָדַיִם		study (masc. sing.)	לוֹמֵד
day	יוֹם		study (fem. sing.)	לוֹמֶדֶת
birthday	יוֹם-הֻלֶּדֶת			

Dictionary מִלּוֹן

ל		Chapter
לִי	to me	
לַיְלָה	night	
לָשׁוֹן	______________	(Intro.)
מ		
מַה, מָה	what?	
מַה שְׁלוֹמְךָ?	______________	(8)
מַה שְׁלוֹמֵךְ?	______________	(8)
מוֹרֶה	teacher (masc. sing.)	
מוֹרָה	teacher (fem. sing.)	
מַזָּל טוֹב	Mazal Tov	
מִי	who?	
מִכְתָּב	______________	(5)
מֶלֶךְ	king	
מְלַמֵּד	______________	(6)
מְלַמֶּדֶת	______________	(6)
מְסִבָּה	______________	(4)
מִשְׁפָּחָה	family	
מָתַי	when?	
מִתְפַּלֵּל	______________	(5)
מִתְפַּלֶּלֶת	______________	(5)
נ		
נוֹתֵן	______________	(5)
נוֹתֶנֶת	______________	(5)
ס		
סַבָּא	______________	(Intro.)
סַבְתָּא	______________	(Intro.)

		Chapter
סִדּוּר	prayer book	
סְלִיחָה	sorry	
סִפּוּר	story	
סֵפֶר	book	
סִפְרִיָּה	library	
סַפְרָנִית	librarian	
ע		
עֲבוֹדָה	______________	(6)
עִבְרִית	Hebrew	
עוֹבֵד	______________	(6)
עוֹבֶדֶת	______________	(6)
עוֹלָם	world	
עוֹמֵד	______________	(Intro.)
עוֹמֶדֶת	______________	(Intro.)
עוֹשֶׂה	______________	(10)
עוֹשָׂה	______________	(10)
עַיִן	______________	(9)
עֵינַיִם	______________	(9)
עַל	on	
עַל-יַד	next to	
עַם יִשְׂרָאֵל	the Jewish people	
עִם	with	
עֵץ	tree	
עֶרֶב	evening	
עֶרֶב טוֹב	good evening	
עֶשֶׂר	ten (fem.)	

Dictionary

מִלוֹן

	Chapter			Chapter	
פ			hear (fem. sing.)		שׁוֹמַעַת
פֶּה	(9)	_____	of, belonging to		שֶׁל
פָּנִים	(9)	_____		(2)	שֶׁלָּה
פֵּרוֹת	fruits			(2)	שֶׁלּוֹ
פְּרִי	fruit			(8)	שָׁלוֹם
צ			three (fem.)		שָׁלוֹשׁ
צְדָקָה	Tzedakah		my		שֶׁלִּי
צִפּוֹר	bird		your (masc. sing.)		שֶׁלְּךָ
ק			your (fem. sing.)		שֶׁלָּךְ
קָדוֹשׁ	(3)	_____	name		שֵׁם
קָטָן	small (masc. sing.)		eight (fem.)		שְׁמוֹנָה
קְטַנָּה	small (fem. sing.)		sun		שֶׁמֶשׁ
ר				(Intro.)	שָׂפָה
רֹאשׁ	head			(Intro.)	שָׂפוֹת
רַבִּי	Rabbi		six (fem.)		שֵׁשׁ
רֶגֶל	(9)	_____	two (amount, fem.)		שְׁתֵּי
רַגְלַיִם	(9)	_____	two (fem.)		שְׁתַּיִם
רוֹאֶה	see (masc. sing.)		**ת**		
רוֹאָה	see (fem. sing.)			(7)	תּוֹדָה
רוֹפֵא	(2)	_____	Torah		תּוֹרָה
רוֹפְאָה	(2)	_____	under		תַּחַת
רְפוּאָה שְׁלֵמָה	(5)	_____	Talmud		תַּלְמוּד
רוֹצֶה	(7)	_____	student (masc. sing.)		תַּלְמִיד
רוֹצָה	(7)	_____	student (fem. sing.)		תַּלְמִידָה
שׁ				(5)	תֵּן
שֶׁבַע	seven (fem.)			(5)	תְּפִלָּה
שַׁבָּת	(4)	_____	nine (fem.)		תֵּשַׁע
שׁוֹמֵעַ	hear (masc. sing.)				